# Instant Vortex
# Air Fryer Oven
# Cookbook for Beginners

**Top 100 Easy to Make and Healthy Oven Recipes to Fry, Bake, Reheat, Dehydrate, and Rotisserie with Your Instant Vortex**

**By Brandi Hatchwell**

# Table of Content

# Introduction

As if helping my little sister prep for a nuptials and seeing her walk down the aisle this past summer wasn't a blessing enough for my family and I, the Instant Pot Company wowed the joy out of me during the same period.

You see, I am a crazy fanatic of cooking devices, food and could travel without much thinking and on a tight budget for the sake of tasting trendy cuisine across seas. I'm not quite sure where this intense love affair began, however, if you will know me, then know me to be a dire enthusiast of food tech.

I have loved my Instant Pot with fair judgements because this device rocks the world of food, making busy life seamless to live. I purchased my IP over three years ago and used it in all its glory without many disappoints. And oh, the Instant Pot found me the love of my life. Talk of a story originated from creamy mustard steak brewed from my Instant Pot (that's one for another day).

Therefore, if the IP Company releases an air fryer that performs multiple functions like it's mother device, what stops me from gifting myself with one. Fast forward to January 2020, I own me one of these devices and my purpose for this cookbook is to share my experience with you while using the Instant Pot Vortex Air Fryer Oven so far –a mouthful, so I will shorten the name to IPVAFO as we proceed.

Here, I combine unadulterated feedback from my usage with one hundred recipes that I have tried, tested, and shared since my purchase (not even a year yet). The recipes follow a straightforward path loaded with meals that are natural to the American cuisine, easy to make, and use easily accessible ingredients.

This collection spreads all hundred recipes into ten comfy categories inspired by my Granny, Mum, Tina (my assistant), my sweet tooth, and ever-hungry tummy. It is a quality of hearty recipes; I urge you to take an intentional walk through the groupings while finding interesting dishes that will feed you all day long and all year long.

We have:

- breakfast and brunch for those super energy kicks in the mornings,
- fish and seafood because why wouldn't we be splurging on the goodness of the sea with a device like this,
- beef, lamb, and pork for all the tasty delicacies they offer for both home cooking and occasions,
- poultry while creating some of the juiciest, crunchiest, and flavor-filled options that I have ever tried,
- desserts because I truly wanted to share those winning, decadent pieces that have had me in all sorts of exciting moments.
- snacks because they are our friendly companion on busy days. Do check out the magic of dehydration of fruit chips like you have never experienced,
- appetizers that are statements for fantastic meals ahead, and
- egg recipes because they deserve an entire category to take away breakfast boredom.

In one word, I'll describe this assemblage as "wonderland at our disposal" because it sits some of Americas choicest hearty meals while giving you the opportunity to make them in the easiest and simplest ways.

Meanwhile, in the following chapters preceding the recipes, I share my fair understanding of the IPVAFO; what it is, it's functions, accessories, and some benefits that I have experienced. The goal, here, is to give you an overview of expectations ahead. On the other hand, if you are knew to this device all together and highly advice having a fill day reading the air fryer's manual to give you a more comprehensive grasp.

To notify, this cookbook isn't a paid review by anyone, but I believe I'm in the right place to declare the device as an essential for homes. Having explored its length and breadth over the last couple of months, I can say that, we are thrilled again with something that cooks Instantly and More Effectively.

Let's cheer to that!

# Chapter 1 The Instant Pot Vortex Air Fryer Oven Basics

## What is Instant Pot Vortex Air Fryer Oven?

**W**hat's that? I recall my exclamation when Tina burst into my office with the good news of the release. Meanwhile, to make things better, Walmart had just done an exclusive release prior to the Prime Day sales.

It was so much of a win for us that day!

I could lose myself talking so much about my experience with this new device but in order to be considerate and lengthy talk, I'll address the topic: **what is this device?**

Air frying is gaining more popularity by the day for its uniqueness to create crispy, healthy foods that play down on excess oil consumption when frying; hence, a wide range of single-functioned air fryers on the market.

Thankfully, the Instant Pot version of the air fryer changes things a bit. It comes along as not only supporting the use of air frying for cooking but also combines the entire function of the oven into its 10-quart petite box. This way, we see a replay of the initial Instant Pot's design with many functions revealing itself in the Air Fryer version.

When I purchased my Air Fryer, I liked the quick and crispier outcome of food that I realized, so much that, I naturally began degrading my oven's presence at mind. Why did the oven have to take so long to make food? I hoped for something better and when the engineers at the IP Company thought alike, and invented a device as an upgrade of the regular air fryer and oven combined, my lot was cast to success (I believe).

The Instant Pot Vortex Air Fryer Oven (I call it IPVAFO) is a faster approach to cooking with implementation of functions like air frying, roasting, baking, re-heating, rotisserie, broiling, and dehydration to make cooking more seamless like you will do on a stovetop or traditional oven. Will the oven be kicked out of time soon? I'm beginning to wonder.

# What Do the Functions Offer?

The IPFAVO offers six functions that culminate into a portable oven. With decent space and access to electrical power, the device works excellently for cooking a wide range of foods.

## Air Frying

Think of buffalo fried chicken, crispy potato backs, etc., this function helps create the crunchiest pieces than regular frying. It offers a cooking temperature range of 180 to 400 F and cooking time range from 1 to 60 minutes with a default cook time of 18 minutes. Based on the recipe at hand, you may adjust the temperature and time setting for your perfect doneness.

## Roasting

What is your favorite recipe to roast in the oven? I love summer vegetable mixes and find this version of the air fryer to make them more tenderly, crispier, and faster than a regular oven will do. Per the recipe's directions, set the temperature between a cooking temperature range of 180 to 400 F and cooking time range from 1 to 60 minutes with a default cook time of 40 minutes.

## Baking

Everything bake-able ranging from cakes, meats and vegetables are perfect for the cook using this function. It allows for a cooking temperature range between 180 to 400 F and cooking time range from 1 to 60 minutes. The best baked dishes are yet to happen in your home.

## Broil

What's better than having the right crust on your cheese topped casseroles or herbed meatloaf? After baking or roasting dishes, this option works best for giving your dish that appealing cheese melt or golden brown crust. While it works great for recipes originally prepared with this device, you may broil other dishes from the stovetop or wherever based on the recipe at hand. It works at a standard temperature for 400 F and cooking time range from 1 to 20 minutes with a default cook time of 8 minutes.

## Reheat

Warm leftovers with this function without drying them out or overcooking them. What better way to enjoy leftovers than this? Place the food in the device, set the temperature between 120 to 360 F and a cooking time range of 1 to 60 minutes with a default cook time of 10 minutes.

## Dehydrate

Check out the snack recipes using this function. I love the outcome a lot! Having tried dehydrating fruits in the oven in the past with disappointments, this device came as a relief. Make dried fruits, vegetables, jerky, etc. with this function using a cooking temperature range of 105 to 160 F with a cooking time range of 1 to 15 hours.

## Rotisserie (using the Roasting Function)

Have you ever dreamed of roasting whole chicken on the rotisserie spit with perfection like that of the restaurants? You just got that magic in your home. To be honest, my first try making rotisserie chicken with this function was my best in comparison to the other first dishes I tried. The skin crisped well with golden brown color and the meat within was juicy, and tender to fall off the bones. Most importantly, since chicken breasts are quick at drying, they surprisingly, turned out soft and very juicy. Cook your favorite whole chicken using the rotisserie spit, Roast mode at a standard temperature of 380 F and cooking timer range of 50 to 70 minutes.

# Accessories for the IPVAFO

The device comes with a set of accessories perfect for its make. Let's have a look at them.

## Drip Pan

This dish traps falling foods or grease while cooking. Open the oven and position the pan at the bottom before adding and cooking foods. This step well followed will serve you the stress of messy drippings.

## Cooking Tray

This tray plays two roles; either as a plate for placing food for cooking or as a platform for placing other dishes like cake pans. You may position this tray on the top or middle racks of the oven before cooking as per the recipe requires. You can use this tray for a wide range of foods depending on the effect sort to achieve.

## Rotisserie Basket

Perfect for air frying small foods, once filled with such foods like chopped potatoes, fries, meat chops, etc., position the basket on the inner lever of the oven and proceed to cook. The basket rotates through the cooking process to ensure that every part of the food is cooked evenly.

## Rotisserie Spit

The spit acts like a regular oven spit for hanging whole chicken during cooking. Run the metal through your prepared whole chicken, close the screws and hang the chicken on the lever in the oven. Proceed to cook as the recipe requires.

## Rotisserie Lift

The lift aids in placing and removing the rotisserie basket and spit when the appliance is hot. Fix the lift at the two ends of the basket or spit and with a little effort, lift the item to your working surface.

# Proven benefits of the IPFAVO

I find that the IP Air Fryer has many similar benefits to the mother Instant Pot and while I still discover more pluses, I will share my first encounters.

## It is Easy and SAfe to Use

With a well-detailed and understandable manual, using the appliance is effortless to use. Once your foods are prepped and placed in the device, proceed to set the temperature and time as the recipe demands. Hit Start and be on your way to experiencing amazing outcomes.

## It Cooks Faster

While this air fryer may not cook as fast as the mother Instant Pot, it sure cooks faster than a regular oven.

## See your Food While it Cooks

The earlier Instant Pot falls short of this benefit because once food is placed into it, covered and begins cooking, you can't observe the outcome until it is done. However, the air fryer has a viewing window with light that can be turned on when you need to look at the food.

## It is Convenient to Use

With the right position for your device, access to electricity, and food to cook, using the air fryer oven is as simple as adding your food, setting the temperature, time, and hitting Start. It is not cumbersome on processes and the manual serves as an excellent guide.

## It Cleans Easily

The accessories that come with the air fryer are made with excellent materials that are easy to clean. Also, when cleaning the inner parts of the device, all you need is damp clothes and good wipe to make it shine line gold.

I bet you're thrilled already to begin using your appliance if you haven't yet. I look forward to the exciting foods that you are yet to make.

Scan though the recipes, make your best choices and let's get cooking!

I am pumped for the food tech industry and the many amazing things being produced like the IPVAFO. Let's share our feedback to drive the positive change!

Cheers,

# Chapter 2 Breakfast & Brunch

## Egg Cheddar Muffins

Prep Time: 10 minutes; Cook time: 15 minutes; Serves: 4

**Ingredients:**
8 large eggs
2 medium carrots, peeled and shredded
1 small orange bell pepper, deseeded and diced
½ cup frozen corn
½ cup frozen peas
Salt and black pepper to taste
¼ cup grated cheddar cheese

**Instructions:**
1. Insert the drip pan at the bottom rack of the device and preheat the air fryer at Bake mode at 350 F for 3 to 4 minutes.
2. Crack the eggs into a medium bowl and whisk in the carrots, bell pepper, corn, peas, salt, black pepper, and half of the cheddar cheese.
3. Lightly grease 6 muffin cups with some olive oil and fill in the egg mixture, two-thirds way up. Top with the remaining cheddar cheese.
4. Open the oven and fit in the cooking tray on the middle rack. Place 3 muffin cups on the tray and close the oven. Set the timer for 15 minutes and cook until the timer reads to the end.
5. Open the lid and check for doneness using a toothpick. If undone, cook further for 5 minutes.
6. Remove the muffins cups and cook the second batch.
7. Serve the egg muffins warm.

**Nutritional Facts Per Serving**
Calories 159, Total Fat 9.36g, Total Carbs 31g, Fiber 2.3g, Protein 7.32g, Sugar 2.79g, Sodium 99mg

# French Toast Sticks with Sugar and Berries

Prep Time: 10 minutes; Cook time: 10 minutes; Serves: 4

**Ingredients:**
4 (2-inch thick) bread slices
2 large eggs
¼ cup whole milk
¼ cup brown sugar
1 tbsp maple syrup
1 tsp cinnamon powder
A pinch nutmeg powder
2 pinches icing sugar for topping
A handful fresh blueberries and raspberries for topping

**Instructions:**
1. Insert the drip pan at the bottom rack of the device and preheat the air fryer at Air Fryer mode at 350 F for 3 to 4 minutes.
2. Cut each bread slice into 4 long strips and set aside.
3. Crack the eggs into a medium bowl and whisk in the milk, maple syrup, cinnamon powder, and nutmeg powder.
4. Place the cooking tray to your side. Working in batches, dip 7 to 8 bread strips into the egg mixture and arrange widthwise on the tray.
5. Open the oven and fit in the cooking tray on the middle rack. Close the oven, set the timer for 10 minutes, and cook until the timer reads to the end.
6. Open the oven, remove the tray and check the toasts, which should not be wet but crispy and sweet.
7. Transfer to serving plates and make the remaining toasts.
8. To serve, sprinkle with the icing sugar and enjoy warm with the berries.

**Nutritional Facts Per Serving**
Calories 132, Total Fat 4g, Total Carbs 17.12g, Fiber 1.7g, Protein 6.77g, Sugar 3.82g, Sodium 190mg

# Tomato Mushroom Frittata

Prep Time: 15 minutes; Cook time: 15 minutes; Serves: 4

**Ingredients:**
1 cup egg white
2 tbsp whole milk
¼ cup sliced tomato
¼ cup sliced mushrooms
2 tbsp chopped fresh chives
Salt and black pepper to taste

**Instructions:**
1. Insert the drip pan at the bottom rack of the device and preheat the air fryer at Bake mode 320 F for 3 to 4 minutes.
2. Lightly grease a 6-inch casserole dish with olive oil, add all the ingredients and whisk until well distributed.
3. Fit the cooking tray on the middle rack of the oven and place the dish on top.
4. Close the oven, set the timer for 15 minutes and bake until the frittata set.
5. Remove from the oven, allow cooling for 2 to 3 minutes, and serve the frittata.

**Nutritional Facts Per Serving**
Calories 93, Total Fat 5.83g, Total Carbs 1.68g, Fiber 0.2g, Protein 7.94g, Sugar 15g, Sodium 87mg

# Potato and Carrot Hashbrowns

Prep Time: 30 minutes; Cook time: 21 minutes; Serves: 4

**Ingredients:**

4 large potatoes, peeled, finely grated, and steamed

1 large carrot, peeled and finely grated

2 tbsp corn flour

Salt and black pepper to taste

1 tsp garlic powder

1 tsp onion powder

2 tsp red chili flakes

2 tsp olive oil, divided

**Instructions:**

1. In a medium bowl, mix all the ingredients except the olive oil until well combined.
2. Oil in the inner part of a 6-inch glass casserole dish with 1 teaspoon of olive oil and spread in the potato mixture. Use a spoon to level the top evenly.
3. Refrigerate the mixture for 20 minutes or until firm.
4. After 20 minutes, insert the drip pan at the bottom rack of the device and preheat the air fryer at Air Fryer mode at 350 F for 3 to 4 minutes.
5. Remove from the dish from the refrigerator; divide the dough into 4 or 6 pieces and shape into rounds.
6. Grease the cooking tray with the remaining olive oil and arrange the hashbrowns patties on top. Fit the cooking tray on the middle rack of the oven and close the oven.
7. Set the timer for 15 minutes and air fry until the timer reads to the end. Open the oven and carefully flip the hashbrowns. Cook further with the timer set for 6 minutes or until uniformly air fried.
8. Open the lid and remove the hashbrowns.
9. Serve warm.

**Nutritional Facts Per Serving**

Calories 334, Total Fat 2.8g, Total Carbs 71.14g, Fiber 9.2g, Protein 8.3g, Sugar 15g, Sodium 37g

# Baked Apples with Pecans

Prep Time: 10 minutes; Cook time: 20 minutes; Serves: 4

**Ingredients:**

4 medium green apples
2 tbsp chopped pecans
2 tbsp raisins
1 ½ tsp melted butter
¼ tsp cinnamon powder
¼ tsp nutmeg powder
¼ cup water

**Instructions:**

1. Preheat the air fryer at Bake mode at 350 F for 3 to 4 minutes.
2. Cut the apples in halves and use a spoon to scoop out some of the flesh from the middle of the fruits. Arrange the apples on the cooking tray and set aside.
3. In a small bowl, mix the pecans, raisins, butter, cinnamon powder, and nutmeg powder. Spoon the mixture into the apple holes.
4. Pour a little water into the drip pan, open the oven, and fit the tray at the bottom of the oven. Also, carefully adjust the tray with the apples on the middle rack and close the oven.
5. Set the timer for 20 minutes and bake until the timer reads to the end.
6. Open the oven and remove the tray with the apples.
7. Allow cooling for 3 minutes and serve warm.

**Nutritional Facts Per Serving**

Calories 134, Total Fat 4.4g, Total Carbs 26g, Fiber 4.8g, Protein 0.83g, Sugar 19.2g, Sodium 2mg

# Puffed Egg Tarts

Prep Time: 10 minutes; Cook time: 32 minutes; Serves: 4

**Ingredients:**

All-purpose flour for dusting

½ (17.3 oz) sheet frozen puff pastry, thawed

¾ cup grated Gruyere cheese, divided

4 large eggs

1 tbsp chopped fresh parsley for garnishing

**Instructions:**

1. Insert the drip pan at the bottom rack of the device and preheat the air fryer at Bake mode at 350 F for 3 to 4 minutes.
2. Lightly dust a clean, flat surface with some flour and roll out the pastry on the surface. Cut into 4 squares and arrange 2 squares on the cooking tray. Insert the tray in the middle rack of the oven, close the device, and bake for 10 minutes or until the pastry is light golden brown.
3. Open the oven, replace the 2 squares with the other 2 squares and bake for 10 minutes too.
4. After, remove the cooking tray and working in batches, place 2 baked squares on top.
5. Use the back of a spoon to press a deep hole into each pastry, divide half of the cheese into the holes of each pastry, and crack an egg onto each.
6. Return the cooking tray to the oven, close the oven and bake for 7 to 11 minutes depending on your desired consistency.
7. Remove from the oven and prepare the remaining squares.
8. To serve, garnish with the parsley and serve immediately.

**Nutritional Facts Per Serving**

Calories 209, Total Fat 14.71g, Total Carbs 3.64g, Fiber 0..1g, Protein 14.9g, Sugar 0.34g, Sodium 266mg

# Crisped Potato Chops

Prep Time: 10 minutes; Cook time: 15 minutes; Serves: 4

**Ingredients:**

5 medium potatoes, peeled and cut to 1-inch cubes
1 tbsp olive oil
Salt and black pepper to taste
½ tsp smoked paprika
½ tsp garlic powder
1 tbsp chopped fresh scallions

**Instructions:**

1. Insert the dripping pan in the bottom part of the air fryer and preheat the oven at Air Fryer mode at 400 F for 2 to 3 minutes.
2. In a medium bowl, mix all the ingredients until well coated.
3. Pour the mixture into the rotisserie basket, cover and lock lid, and insert the basket into the oven using the rotisserie lift.
4. Close the oven and cook in the potatoes at a time setting of 15 minutes while stopping and shaking the basket every 2 to 3 minutes until the potatoes are golden brown, crisp, and tender.
5. Open the oven and transfer the potatoes to a plate.
6. Garnish with the scallions and serve warm.

**Nutritional Facts Per Serving**

Calories 242, Total Fat 3.68g, Total Carbs 48.14g, Fiber 6.2g, Protein 5.74g, Sugar 2.73g, Sodium 18mg

# Meaty Scotch Eggs

Prep Time: 15 minutes; Cook time: 15 minutes; Serves: 4

**Ingredients:**

1 lb. crumbled uncooked sausage
8 hard-boiled eggs
1-2 raw eggs
1 cup crushed pork rinds (salt-seasoned)
1 tbsp olive oil for greasing
1 tbsp chopped fresh chives

**Instructions:**

1. Insert the dripping pan in the bottom part of the air fryer and preheat the oven at Air Fryer mode at 400 F for 2 to 3 minutes.
2. Meanwhile, create 8 flat patties out of the sausage and generously wrap each boiled egg with each patty until well covered.
3. Crack and beat the raw eggs in a small bowl and set aside. Pour the pork rinds into a shallow plate and set aside too. Also, lightly brush the rotisserie basket with some olive oil and let sit by you.
4. Carefully roll the meat covered eggs in the beaten eggs, coat all around in the pork rinds, and repeat the coating process a second time.
7. Arrange the eggs in the rotisserie basket, cover and lock lid, and insert the basket into the oven using the rotisserie lift.
5. Close the oven and set the timer 15 minutes. Cook until the egg coating is golden brown.
6. Open the oven, transfer from serving plates, cut into halves, and garnish with the chives.
7. Serve warm.

**Nutritional Facts Per Serving**

Calories 614, Total Fat 45.13g, Total Carbs 13.34g, Fiber 3.2g, Protein 42.63g, Sugar 1.38g, Sodium 1238mg

# Caramelized Bananas

Prep Time: 10 minutes; Cook time: 6 minutes; Serves: 4

**Ingredients:**

2 medium bananas

¼ lemon, juiced

1 tbsp brown sugar

½ tsp cinnamon powder

**For topping:**

¼ cup Greek yogurt

2 tbsp chopped toasted nuts (of your choice)

**Instructions:**

1. Insert the dripping pan in the bottom part of the air fryer and preheat the oven at Bake mode at 400 F for 2 to 3 minutes.
2. Peel the bananas and slice in half lengthwise. Drizzle the lemon juice on the bananas, followed by the brown sugar and cinnamon powder.
3. Arrange the bananas on the cooking tray, insert onto the middle rack of the oven, and close the oven.
4. Set the timer for 6 minutes and bake until the timer reads to the end.
5. Transfer the bananas to serving plates and top with the yogurt and nuts.
6. Serve immediately.

**Nutritional Facts Per Serving**

Calories 61, Total Fat 0.33g, Total Carbs 14.4g, Fiber 1.7g, Protein 1.77g, Sugar 7.7g, Sodium 5mg

# Egg and Bacon Cups

Prep Time: 10 minutes; Cook time: 13 minutes; Serves: 4

## Ingredients:
4 bread slices
2 bacon slices, cooked and chopped
4 large eggs
Salt and black pepper to taste

## Instructions:
1. Insert the dripping pan in the bottom part of the air fryer and preheat the oven at Bake mode at 400 F for 2 to 3 minutes.
2. Fit each bread slice into each of 4 medium muffin cups to form cups and divide the bacon into each. Crack the eggs into the cups, season with salt, black pepper, and place the cups on the cooking tray.
3. Insert the cooking tray onto the middle rack of the oven, close the air fryer, and bake in the oven 13 minutes.
4. Once ready, remove from the oven, take the food out of the cups, and serve immediately.

## Nutritional Facts Per Serving
Calories 202, Total Fat 10.82g, Total Carbs 15.56g, Fiber 1.3g, Protein 11.24g, Sugar 2.58g, Sodium 280mg

# Chapter 3 Appetizers

## Bacon Wrapped Smokies

Prep Time: 15 minutes; Cook time: 25 minutes; Serves: 4

**Ingredients:**
1 lb. thin bacon slices
1 package (14 oz) little smoked sausages
1 cup brown sugar

**Instructions:**
1. Insert the dripping pan at the bottom of the air fryer and preheat in Air Fry mode at 350 F for 2 to 3 minutes.
2. Wrap the bacon slices around the each sausage and secure with toothpick. Lay as much wrapped sausage as possible on the cooking tray and sprinkle with the brown sugar.
3. Slide the cooking tray onto the middle rack of the air fryer and close the lid.
4. Set the timer for 25 minutes and press Start. Cook until the sugar melts and the food is golden brown.
5. Transfer this batch to a serving platter and make the remaining.
6. Serve warm.

**Nutrition Facts Per Serving**
Calories 559, Total Fat 44.53g, Total Carbs 25.88g, Fiber 0g, Protein 14.21g, Sugar 25.39g, Sodium 533mg

# Pancetta and Cheese Jalapeno Poppers

Prep Time: 10 minutes; Cook time: 18 minutes; Serves: 4

**Ingredients:**
6 oz light cream cheese
½ cup Monterey Jack cheese
2 small scallions, chopped
½ garlic powder
Salt to taste
12 jalapeno peppers, halved lengthwise and deseeded
4 pancetta slices, cooked and chopped
½ cup panko breadcrumbs
Nonstick cooking spray

**Instructions:**
1. Insert the dripping pan at the bottom of the air fryer and preheat in Air Fry mode at 350 F for 2 to 3 minutes.
2. In a medium bowl, mix the cream cheese, Monterey jack cheese, scallions, garlic powder, and salt. Fill the mixture into the jalapeno peppers, top with the pancetta, breadcrumbs, and grease lightly with cooking spray.
3. Working in batches, arrange the peppers on the cooking tray, slide the cooking tray onto the middle rack of the air fryer and close the lid.
4. Set the timer for 18 minutes and press Start. Cook until the cheese melts and is golden brown on top.
5. Transfer this batch to a serving platter and make the remaining.
6. Serve warm.

**Nutrition Facts Per Serving**
Calories 227, Total Fat 18.93g, Total Carbs 5.15g, Fiber 1.2g, Protein 9.98g, Sugar 3.67g, Sodium 386mg

# Gingered Bacon Wrapped Scallops

Prep Time: 10 minutes; Cook time: 15 minutes; Serves: 6

**Ingredients:**

¼ cup tamarind sauce

1 tbsp dark brown sugar

1 ½ tsp minced fresh ginger

6 very large "dry" sea scallops

6 slices bacon, cut in half crosswise

**Instructions:**

1. Insert the dripping pan at the bottom of the air fryer and preheat in Air Fry mode at 350 F for 2 to 3 minutes.
2. In a medium bowl, mix the tamarind sauce, brown sugar, ginger, and scallops. Allow marinating for 15 minutes and then, wrap each scallop with two bacon slices. Secure with toothpicks. Arrange the wrapped scallops on the cooking tray.
3. Slide the cooking tray onto the middle rack of the air fryer and close the lid.
4. Set the timer for 15 minutes and press Start. Cook until the bacon is golden brown and crispy whole turning the food halfway the cooking time.
5. Transfer to a serving platter and serve warm.

**Nutrition Facts Per Serving**

Calories 164, Total Fat 15.35g, Total Carbs 1.55g, Fiber 0.3g, Protein 5.15g, Sugar 0.98g, Sodium 258mg

# Tomato Bruschetta

Prep Time: 10 minutes; Cook time: 15 minutes; Serves: 2

**Ingredients:**

8 medium baguette slices

2 garlic cloves, halved

2 (28 oz) cans peeled whole tomatoes, drained and chopped

Salt to taste

¼ cup olive oil + more for drizzling

15 large basil leaves, thinly sliced into a chiffonade

2 tbsp red wine vinegar to taste

Granulated sugar to taste

**Instructions:**

1. Insert the dripping pan at the bottom of the air fryer and preheat in Air Fry mode at 350 F for 2 to 3 minutes.
2. Brush the baguette slices on both sides with the garlic halves, some olive oil and arrange on the cooking tray.
3. Slide the cooking tray onto the middle rack of the air fryer and close the lid.
4. Set the timer for 15 minutes and press Start. Cook until the bread is crispy and golden brown.
5. Meanwhile, in a medium bowl, mix the remaining ingredients and allow sitting to incorporate flavors while the bread gets ready.
6. To serve, lay the bread slices on a flat surface and top with the tomato mixture. Enjoy immediately.

**Nutrition Facts Per Serving**

Calories 176, Total Fat 9.97g, Total Carbs 16.33g, Fiber 8g, Protein 8.45g, Sugar 11.35g, Sodium 799mg

# Crispy Potato Skins

Prep Time: 15 minutes; Cook time: 15 minutes; Serves: 4

## Ingredients:

5 small potatoes, baked
2 tbsp unsalted butter, melted
¼ tsp salt
¼ tsp garlic powder
3 bacon slices, cooked and crumbled
2 tbsp chopped fresh chives
1 cup grated cheddar cheese
1 cup sour cream for serving

## Instructions:

1. Insert the dripping pan at the bottom of the air fryer and preheat in Air Fry mode at 400 F for 2 to 3 minutes.
2. Cut the potatoes into 4 quarters, scoop off most of the flesh and brush the skin with the butter on both sides. Season with the salt and garlic powder.
3. Arrange the skins on the cooking tray, slide the tray onto the middle rack of the air fryer and close the lid.
4. Set the timer for 15 minutes and press Start. Cook until the skins are crispy turning halfway.
5. To serve, top the inner part of each flesh with the bacon, chives, cheddar cheese, and sour cream. Enjoy.

## Nutrition Facts Per Serving

Calories 575, Total Fat 20.05g, Total Carbs 84.98g, Fiber 10.2g, Protein 16.1g, Sugar 3.96g, Sodium 308mg

# Baked Pears with Blue Cheese and Honey

Prep Time: 10 minutes; Cook time: 10 minutes; Serves: 4

**Ingredients:**

1 tbsp melted butter for greasing

4 ripe pears, halves and cored

1 tbsp chopped fresh thyme + more for topping

1 tbsp honey

6 tsp soft blue cheese

Salt and black pepper to taste

Chopped pecans to garnish

**Instructions:**

1. Insert the dripping pan at the bottom of the air fryer and preheat in Bake mode at 400 F for 2 to 3 minutes. Lightly grease a 6-inch baking dish with melted butter.
2. Use a spoon to create a shallow hole at the center of each pear half and top with the thyme and honey. Arrange the pears in the baking dish with open side up.
3. Slide the cooking tray upside down onto the middle rack of the air fryer, sit the baking dish on top and close the lid.
4. Set the timer for 10 minutes and press Start. Cook until the pears soften and are golden brown.
5. Remove from the oven when ready and to serve, transfer the pears to plate and spoon the blue cheese at the center of the pears. Season with salt, black pepper, add the pecans, and drizzle with some honey.
6. Enjoy!

**Nutrition Facts Per Serving**

Calories 235, Total Fat 22.52g, Total Carbs 9.32g, Fiber 2.9g, Protein 2.8g, Sugar 5.97g, Sodium 24mg

# Mac and Cheese Mini Cups

Prep Time: 12 minutes; Cook time: 15 minutes; Serves: 4

**Ingredients:**

8 oz elbow macaroni, cooked

2 tbsp salted butter, melted + more for greasing

¼ tsp paprika

2 tbsp plain flour

½ cup whole milk

8 oz grated sharp cheddar cheese

1 tbsp chopped fresh chives

**Instructions:**

1. Preheat the device in Bake mode at 400 F for 2 to 3 minutes and lightly grease an 8-holed muffin tray with melted butter.
2. Add all the ingredients to a bowl and mix well. Spoon the mixture into the muffin cups making sure to press to fit.
3. Slide the cooking tray upside down onto the middle rack of the air fryer, sit the muffin dish on top and close the lid.
4. Set the timer for 15 minutes and press Start. Cook until the golden brown on top and the cheese melted.
5. Remove the muffin tray from the oven, allow cooling until the cheese firms a bit and remove the food.
6. Serve warm.

**Nutrition Facts Per Serving**

Calories 386, Total Fat 10.7g, Total Carbs 55.44g, Fiber 2g, Protein 16.39g, Sugar 9.48g, Sodium 673mg

# Baked Tomatoes with Parmesan and Mozzarella

Prep Time: 10 minutes; Cook time: 10 minutes; Serves: 4

## Ingredients:

4 roma tomatoes, halved
1 cup grated Parmesan cheese
1 cup grated mozzarella cheese
½ cup chopped fresh basil
Olive oil for drizzling

## Instructions:

1. Insert the dripping pan at the bottom of the air fryer and preheat in Bake mode at 400 F for 2 to 3 minutes.
2. Arrange the tomato halves on the cooking tray with open side facing up and fill with the cheese and basil.
3. Slide the tray onto the middle rack of the air fryer and close the lid.
4. Set the timer for 10 minutes and press Start. Cook until the cheese melts and is bubbly.
5. Remove the tray from the oven, allow sitting for 2 minutes and serve afterwards.

## Nutrition Facts Per Serving

Calories 933, Total Fat 7.23g, Total Carbs 9.33g, Fiber 2g, Protein 17.24g, Sugar 3.68g, Sodium 667mg

# Loaded Potato Bites

Prep Time: 10 minutes; Cook time: 15 minutes; Serves: 4

## Ingredients:

3 russet potatoes, cleaned and cut into 1-inch rounds
¼ cup butter
¼ cup chopped scallions
1 cup grated cheddar cheese
3 tbsp chopped and cooked bacon bits

## Instructions:

1. Insert the dripping pan at the bottom of the air fryer and preheat in Bake mode at 400 F for 2 to 3 minutes.
2. Arrange the potato pieces on the cooking tray, spread the butter on top and top with the scallions and cheese.
3. Slide the tray onto the middle rack of the air fryer and close the lid.
4. Set the timer for 15 minutes and press Start. Cook until the cheese melts and is bubbly.
5. Remove the tray from the oven, allow sitting for 2 minutes, garnish with the bacon, and serve afterwards.

## Nutrition Facts Per Serving

Calories 347, Total Fat 13.11g, Total Carbs 51.98g, Fiber 4.3g, Protein 7.84g, Sugar 1.87g, Sodium 199mg

# Bacon Wrapped Asparagus

Prep Time: 10 minutes; Cook time: 15 minutes; Serves: 4

## Ingredients:

24 stalks asparagus, hard ends trimmed
12 slices bacon
Garlic salt and black pepper to taste

## Instructions:

1. Insert the dripping pan at the bottom of the air fryer and preheat in Air Fry mode at 400 F for 2 to 3 minutes.
2. Wrap each of two asparagus from top to bottom with one bacon slice and lay lengthwise on the cooking tray. Season with the garlic salt and black pepper.
3. Slide the cooking tray onto the middle rack of the air fryer and close the lid.
4. Set the timer for 15 minutes and press Start. Cook until the bacon is crispy.
5. Remove the tray from the oven, allow sitting for 2 minutes, and serve.

## Nutrition Facts Per Serving

Calories 644, Total Fat 61.31g, Total Carbs 3.42g, Fiber 0.3g, Protein 20g, Sugar 2.44g, Sodium 735mg

# Chapter 4 Eggs

## Chili Scramble Eggs

Prep Time: 10 minutes; Cook time: 10 minutes; Serves: 4

**Ingredients:**

18 eggs

3 tbsp butter

3 tbsp flour

¾ tsp salt

1½ cups heavy cream

Salt and black pepper to taste

¼ tsp red chili flakes

**Instructions:**

1. Preheat the air fryer oven in Bake mode at 375 F for 2 to 3 minutes and lightly grease a baking pan with cooking spray. Set aside.
2. In a medium bowl, crack the eggs and whisk with the butter, flour, salt, heavy cream, salt, black pepper, and red chili flakes. Beat until creamy and fluffy.
3. Pour the egg mixture into the cake pan. Slide the cooking tray upside down onto the middle rack, place the baking pan on top and close the oven.
4. Set the timer for 10 minutes and press Start. Cook until the eggs solidify while mixing the eggs thoroughly every 2 minutes.
5. Remove the food from the oven when ready and serve warm.

**Nutrition Facts Per Serving**

Calories 841, Total Fat 68.77g, Total Carbs 11.44g, Fiber 0.4g, Protein 42.22g, Sugar 4.79g, Sodium 987mg

# Simple Baked Eggs with Tomatoes

Prep Time: 10 minutes; Cook time: 15 minutes; Serves: 4

**Ingredients:**

1 tbsp butter + extra for greasing

½ small yellow onion, chopped

2 garlic cloves, minced

Salt and black pepper to taste

1 tsp smoked paprika

14 oz crushed tomatoes

4 eggs

1 tbsp chopped fresh oregano to garnish

**Instructions:**

1. Preheat the air fryer oven in Bake mode at 350 F for 2 to 3 minutes and lightly grease 6-inch baking dish with butter.
2. Melt the butter in a medium skillet and sauté the onion until softened, 3 minutes. Add the garlic, cook for 30 seconds or until fragrant and season with salt, and black pepper. Mix in the tomatoes and simmer the sauce until thickened.
3. Transfer the sauce to the baking pan, crack the eggs on top and scatter the oregano on top.
4. Slide the cooking tray upside down onto the middle rack, place the baking pan on top and close the oven.
5. Set the timer for 10 minutes and press Start. Cook until the eggs whites set but the yolks still runny.
6. Remove the food from the oven when ready and serve warm.

**Nutrition Facts Per Serving**

Calories 194, Total Fat 13.99g, Total Carbs 6.9g, Fiber 1.5g, Protein 10.65g, Sugar 1.75g, Sodium 169mg

# Classic Western Omelet

Prep Time: 5 minutes; Cook time: 10 minutes; Serves: 4

## Ingredients:

8 eggs

1 cup whole milk

Salt and black pepper to taste

1 medium red bell pepper, deseeded and chopped

1 medium green bell pepper, deseeded and chopped

¾ cup chopped cooked ham

½ cup chopped scallions

½ tbsp chopped fresh chives

½ cup grated cheddar cheese

## Instructions:

1. Preheat the air fryer oven in Bake mode at 350 F for 2 to 3 minutes and lightly grease 6-inch baking dish with butter.
2. In a medium bowl, crack the eggs and whisk well with the remaining ingredients. Pour the egg mixture into cake pan making sure that the vegetables are well distributed.
3. Slide the cooking tray upside down onto the middle rack, place the baking pan on top and close the oven.
4. Set the timer for 10 minutes and press Start. Cook until the omelet sets and is cooked within.
5. Remove the pan after, allow cooling for 1 minute, slice and serve warm.

## Nutrition Facts Per Serving

Calories 336, Total Fat 21.31g, Total Carbs 14.76g, Fiber 1.3g, Protein 20.73g, Sugar 11.83g, Sodium 236mg

# Baked Eggs in Avocado

Prep Time: 10 minutes; Cook time: 10 minutes; Serves: 4

**Ingredients:**
2 avocados, halved and pitted
2 large eggs
Salt and black pepper to taste
2 tbsp chopped fresh parsley

**Instructions:**
1. Preheat the air fryer oven in Bake mode at 350 F for 2 to 3 minutes.
2. Working in batches, place the avocado on the cooking tray with the hole side facing up, and crack an egg into each. Season with salt and black pepper.
3. Carefully, slide the cooking tray upside down onto the middle rack and close the oven.
4. Set the timer for 10 minutes and press Start. Cook until the egg whites set but the yolk still runny.
5. Remove the first batch from the oven and prepare the second set of avocados with eggs.
6. To serve, garnish with the parsley and serve immediately with bread.

**Nutrition Facts Per Serving**
Calories 193, Total Fat 17.03g, Total Carbs 10.06g, Fiber 7g, Protein 3.64g, Sugar 1.3g, Sodium 13mg

# Cheesy Baked Eggs

Prep Time: 15 minutes; Cook time: 15 minutes; Serves: 4

## Ingredients:

1 tbsp butter, melted

12 eggs, beaten

1 cup grated Monterey Jack cheese

1 cup grated Parmesan cheese

½ cup all-purpose flour

1 tsp salt

## Instructions:

1. Preheat the air fryer oven in Bake mode at 350 F for 2 to 3 minutes and lightly grease 6-inch baking dish with butter.
2. In a medium bowl, whisk the eggs with the remaining butter, cheeses, flour, and salt. Pour the mixture into the baking dish.
3. Slide the cooking tray upside down onto the middle rack, place the baking pan on top and close the oven.
4. Set the timer for 15 minutes and press Start. Cook until the egg sets and is cooked within.
5. Remove the pan after, allow cooling for 1 minute, slice and serve warm.

## Nutrition Facts Per Serving

Calories 699, Total Fat 48.9g, Total Carbs 18.67g, Fiber 0.4g, Protein 43.73g, Sugar 2.18g, Sodium 1560mg

# Bacon, Veggie and Egg Muffins

Prep Time: 10 minutes; Cook time: 15 minutes; Serves: 4

## Ingredients:

8 large eggs
2 bacon slices, chopped and cooked
A handful frozen mixed veggies, not thawed
Salt and black pepper to taste
¼ cup grated pepper jack cheese

## Instructions:

1. Insert the drip pan at the bottom rack of the device and preheat the air fryer in Bake mode at 350 F for 3 to 4 minutes.
2. Crack the eggs into a medium bowl and whisk in the remaining ingredients until well combined.
3. Lightly grease 6 muffin cups with some olive oil and fill in the egg mixture, two-thirds way up. Top with the remaining cheddar cheese.
4. Open the oven and fit in the cooking tray on the middle rack. Place 3 muffin cups on the tray and close the oven. Set the timer for 15 minutes and cook until the timer reads to the end.
5. Open the lid and check for doneness using a toothpick. If undone, cook further for 5 minutes.
6. Remove the muffins cups and cook the second batch.
7. Serve the egg muffins warm.

## Nutrition Facts Per Serving

Calories 198, Total Fat 16.65g, Total Carbs 2.45g, Fiber 0.2g, Protein 9.27g, Sugar 0.91g, Sodium 128mg

# Cheese and Ham Eggs Baked in Toast

Prep Time: 5 minutes; Cook time: 8 minutes; Serves: 4

**Ingredients:**

1 tbsp butter for spreading

4 slices white bread

4 eggs, room temperature

¼ cup cubed precooked ham

¼ cup shredded Monterey Jack cheese

1 tbsp chopped fresh parsley for garnishing

**Instructions:**

1. Preheat the air fryer oven in Bake mode at 375 F for 2 to 3 minutes and lightly grease 6-inch cooking tray with a little butter.
2. Arrange the bread slices on the cooking tray, scoop out holes from the center of each bread while make sure to have little bread lining at the bottom, and spread the butter on the top side of the bread.
3. Crack an egg into each hole and add the ham, cheese, and parsley. Season with salt and black pepper.
4. Slide the cooking tray onto the middle rack and close the oven.
5. Set the timer for 8 minutes and press Start. Cook until the egg whites set and the yolks still runny.
6. Transfer the dish to serving plates and enjoy immediately.

**Nutrition Facts Per Serving**

Calories 253, Total Fat 15.63g, Total Carbs 13.43g, Fiber 2.6g, Protein 14.03g, Sugar 2.1g, Sodium 309mg

# Idaho Sunrise

Prep Time: 8 minutes; Cook time: 25 minutes; Serves: 2

**Ingredients:**

2 large Russet potatoes, mostly baked

1 tbsp butter

2 eggs

2 prosciutto slices, cooked and crumbled

2 tbsp grated Gouda cheese

1 tbsp fresh parsley, chopped

Salt and black pepper to taste

**Instructions:**

1. Preheat the air fryer oven in Bake mode at 350 F for 2 to 3 minutes.
2. Lay the potatoes on the side on the cooking tray, cut off a ¼ -inch off the top, and use a spoon to scoop out some of the flesh to create a cup.
3. Divide the butter in the middle of each potatoes, crack an egg into each and add the prosciutto, Gouda cheese, parsley, salt, and black pepper. care
4. Slide the cooking tray onto the middle rack and close the oven.
5. Set the timer for 25 minutes and press Start. Cook until the egg whites set and the yolks still runny.
6. Transfer the dish to serving plates and enjoy immediately.

**Nutrition Facts Per Serving**

Calories 276, Total Fat 10.27g, Total Carbs 35.95g, Fiber 2.6g, Protein 11.21g, Sugar 2.77g, Sodium 258mg

# Spinach Eggs Florentine

Prep Time: 10 minutes; Cook time: 25 minutes; Serves: 4

**Ingredients:**

3 tbsp melted butter

1 slice bread, torn into rough bits

Salt and black pepper

2 tsp chopped fresh thyme leaves

1 large shallot, minced

2 garlic cloves, minced

1 ½ cups chopped spinach

4 large eggs

½ cup coconut or heavy cream

1 tbsp chopped fresh sage

A pinch nutmeg powder

**Instructions:**

1. Preheat the air fryer oven in Bake mode at 375 F for 2 to 3 minutes and lightly grease 6-inch baking dish with a little butter. Set aside.
2. Melt a tbsp butter in medium skillet and stir-fry the bread until golden brown and crispy, 10 minutes. Season with a little salt, black pepper, and thyme. Transfer to a plate and set aside.
3. Melt the remaining butter in the skillet and sauté the shallot and garlic until softened and fragrant, 2 minutes. Mix in the spinach to wilt and season with salt and black pepper.
4. Transfer to the baking dish, create separate four holes in the spinach, and crack an egg into each. Pour the coconut cream around the eggs, top with the sage, season with salt, black pepper, nutmeg, and sprinkle the bread mixture on top.
5. Slide the cooking tray onto the middle rack, place the baking dish on top and close the oven.
6. Set the timer for 15 minutes and press Start. Cook until the egg whites set and the yolks still runny.
7. Transfer the dish to serving plates and enjoy immediately.

**Nutrition Facts Per Serving**

Calories 208, Total Fat 19.02g, Total Carbs 5.93g, Fiber 0.9g, Protein 4.2g, Sugar 1.68g, Sodium 160mg

# Kale Parmesan Frittata

Prep Time: 15 minutes; Cook time: 15 minutes; Serves: 4

## Ingredients:
1 cup egg white
2 tbsp whole milk
¼ cup chopped kale
¼ cup sliced mushrooms
2 tbsp chopped fresh chives
Salt and black pepper to taste
1 cup grated Parmesan cheese

## Instructions:
1. Insert the drip pan at the bottom rack of the device and preheat the air fryer in Bake mode at 320 F for 3 to 4 minutes.
2. Lightly grease a 6-inch casserole dish with olive oil, add all the ingredients and whisk until well distributed.
3. Fit the cooking tray on the middle rack of the oven and place the dish on top. Closer the oven.
4. Select Bake mode, set the timer for 15 minutes and bake until the frittata is set.
5. Remove from the oven, allow cooling for 2 to 3 minutes and serve the frittata.

## Nutrition Facts Per Serving
Calories 142, Total Fat 7.11g, Total Carbs 5.15g, Fiber 0.2g, Protein 14.06g, Sugar 1.08g, Sodium 553mg

# Chapter 5 Fish & Seafood

## Fish Tacos

Prep Time: 10 minutes; Cook time: 9 minutes; Serves: 4

**Ingredients:**
4 cod fillets, cut into 1-inch cubes
Salt and black pepper to taste
½ lime, juiced
½ cup all-purpose flour
1 large egg, lightly beaten
1 cup panko breadcrumbs
Olive oil for brushing
4 medium corn tortillas
½ cup shredded red cabbage
1 medium avocado, pitted, peeled, and chopped
2 tbsp chopped fresh cilantro
1 cup sour cream
Lime wedges for serving

**Instructions:**
1. Insert the dripping pan in the bottom part of the air fryer and preheat the oven at Air Fry mode at 400 F for 2 to 3 minutes. Lightly brush the rotisserie basket with some olive oil and set aside.
2. Season the fish with salt, black pepper, and lime juice.
3. Pour the flour onto a plate and the breadcrumbs onto another. Dredge the fish pieces lightly on the flour, then in the eggs, and the breadcrumbs. Put the coated fish in the rotisserie basket and fit into the oven using the rotisserie lift.
4. Set the timer for 9 minutes or until the fish pieces are golden brown.
5. To serve, lay the tortillas individually on a clean, flat surface and add the fish pieces. Top with the cabbage, avocado, cilantro, sour cream, and lime wedges.
6. Serve immediately.

**Nutritional Facts Per Serving**
Calories 275, Total Fat 11.34g, Total Carbs 19.39g, Fiber 25g, Protein 23.37g, Sugar 1.5g, Sodium 422mg

# Asian Coconut Shrimp

Prep Time: 10 minutes; Cook time: 8 minutes; Serves: 4

## Ingredients:
½ cup all-purpose flour
2 large eggs
2/3 cup unsweetened coconut flakes
1/3 cup panko breadcrumbs
24 medium shrimps
Salt and black pepper to taste
Olive oil

## Instructions:
1. Insert the dripping pan in the bottom part of the air fryer and preheat the oven at Air Fry mode at 400 F for 2 to 3 minutes. Lightly brush the rotisserie basket with some olive oil and set aside.
2. Pour the flour into a shallow plate, whisk the eggs in a bowl, and mix the coconut flakes with breadcrumbs on another plate.
3. Season the shrimps with salt, black pepper, and dredge lightly in the flour. Proceed to coat in the eggs and then, generously, in the breadcrumbs mixture.
4. Spray the coated shrimps with some olive oil and arrange it in the rotisserie basket. Fit the basket in the oven using the rotisserie lift and set the timer for 8 minutes or until the shrimps are golden brown.
5. When ready, transfer the shrimps to serving plates and serve warm with sweet coconut dipping sauce.

## Nutritional Facts Per Serving
Calories 190, Total Fat 7.16g, Total Carbs 20.88g, Fiber 2g, Protein 10.32g, Sugar 5.95g, Sodium 281mg

# Mahi Mahi with Herby Buttery Drizzle

Prep Time: 10 minutes; Cook time: 12 minutes; Serves: 4

**Ingredients:**
4 (6 oz) Mahi Mahi fillets
Salt and black pepper to taste
Olive oil for spraying
2/3 cup butter, melted
1 tbsp chopped fresh parsley
½ tbsp chopped fresh dill

**Instructions:**
1. Insert the dripping pan in the bottom part of the air fryer and preheat the oven at Bake mode at 400 F for 2 to 3 minutes.
2. Season the Mahi Mahi fillets with salt, black pepper, and grease lightly with some olive oil. Lay the fish on the cooking tray and fit onto the middle rack of the oven.
3. Close the lid and set the timer for 12 minutes.
4. Once the fish cooks, transfer to a serving platter. Whisk the butter with the parsley and dill, and drizzle the mixture on the fish before serving.
5. Enjoy immediately.

**Nutritional Facts Per Serving**
Calories 529, Total Fat 46.54g, Total Carbs 9.25g, Fiber 5.6g, Protein 20.26g, Sugar 1.28g, Sodium 422mg

# Classic Lemon Pepper Haddock

Prep Time: 10 minutes; Cook time: 12 minutes; Serves: 4

## Ingredients:

¼ cup all-purpose flour
2 egg whites
1/3 cup panko breadcrumbs
2 tsp lemon pepper
2 egg whites
4 (8 oz) haddock fillets
Salt to taste
2 slices lemon
Chopped parsley to garnish

## Instructions:

1. Insert the dripping pan in the bottom part of the air fryer and preheat the oven at Air Fry mode at 400 F for 2 to 3 minutes.
2. Pour the flour in a shallow plate, mix the breadcrumbs and lemon peppers in another shallow dish, whisk the egg whites lightly in a medium bowl, and season the fish lightly with salt.
3. Dredge the fish lightly in the flour, then coat in the egg whites, and then generously in the breadcrumbs mixture.
4. Lay the fish on the cooking tray, grease lightly with cooking spray, and fit onto the middle rack of the oven. Close the air fryer and set the timer for 12 minutes.
5. Once the fish cooks, transfer to a serving platter and serve immediately with the lemon and parsley garnish.

## Nutritional Facts Per Serving

Calories 208, Total Fat 1.22g, Total Carbs 10.95g, Fiber 1.1g, Protein 36.88g, Sugar 2.14g, Sodium 476mg

# Fried Scallops with Saffron Cream Sauce

Prep Time: 5 minutes; Cook time: 2 minutes; Serves: 4

**Ingredients:**

Olive oil for greasing
24 scallops, cleaned
2/3 cup heavy cream
1 tbsp freshly squeezed lemon juice
¼ tsp dried crushed saffron threads

**Instructions:**

1. Insert the dripping pan in the bottom part of the air fryer and preheat the oven at Air Fry mode 400 F for 2 to 3 minutes.
2. Lightly brush the rotisserie basket with some olive oil and fill with the scallops.
3. Close and fit the basket in the oven using the rotisserie lift and set the timer for 2 minutes or until the scallops are golden brown on the outside.
4. Meanwhile, in a medium bowl, quickly whisk the heavy cream lemon juice and saffron threads.
5. When the scallops are ready, transfer to a serving plate and drizzle the sauce on top.
6. Enjoy immediately.

**Nutritional Facts Per Serving**

Calories 77, Total Fat 7.73g, Total Carbs 1.05g, Fiber 0g, Protein 1.15g, Sugar 0.66g, Sodium 31mg

# Easy Crab Cakes

Prep Time: 10 minutes; Cook time: 10 minutes; Serves: 4

## Ingredients:

8 oz lump crab
1 medium red bell pepper, deseeded and diced
2 scallions, finely chopped
2 tbsp mayonnaise
2 tbsp panko bread crumbs
1 tbsp Dijon mustard
1 tsp old bay seasoning
Olive oil for spraying
4 lemon wedges for serving

## Instructions:

1. Insert the dripping pan in the bottom part of the air fryer and preheat the oven at Bake mode at 370 F for 2 to 3 minutes.
2. Meanwhile, in a medium bowl, mix all the ingredients except for the olive oil and lemon wedges until evenly distributed. Form 4 to 6 firm patties from the mixture, arrange on the cooking tray, and grease lightly with some olive oil. You may do this in two batches.
3. Fit the cooking tray on the middle rack and close the oven. Set the timer to 10 minutes and cook until the timer reads to the end, and the crab cakes are golden brown and well compacted.
4. Remove the crab cakes from the oven and serve with the lemon wedges.

## Nutritional Facts Per Serving

Calories 246, Total Fat 6.19g, Total Carbs 13.65g, Fiber 1.5g, Protein 33.16g, Sugar 3.65g, Sodium 338mg

# Sweet Asian Style Salmon

Prep Time: 10 minutes; Cook time: 12 minutes; Serves: 4

**Ingredients:**

2 garlic cloves, minced

1 tbsp fresh ginger paste

2 tsp fresh orange zest

½ cup fresh orange juice

¼ cup soy sauce

3 tbsp plain vinegar

1 tbsp olive oil

Salt to taste

4 (5 oz) salmon fillets

**Instructions:**

1. In a large bowl, mix all the ingredients except for the fish and place the fish in the sauce. Spoon the sauce well on top and cover the bowl with a plastic wrap. Allow marinating at room temperature for 30 minutes.
2. After 30 minutes, insert the dripping pan in the bottom part of the air fryer and preheat the oven at Bake mode at 400 F for 2 to 3 minutes.
3. Using tongs, remove the fish from the sauce, making sure to shake off some marinade of the fish and place the cooking tray. You can work in two batches.
4. Slide the tray onto the top rack of the oven, close the oven, and set the timer for 12 minutes, flipping the fish after 6 minutes.
5. Once ready, transfer the fish to serving plates and serve warm with steamed greens.

**Nutritional Facts Per Serving**

Calories 132, Total Fat 7.39g, Total Carbs 8.72g, Fiber 0.5g, Protein 7.2g, Sugar 5.96g, Sodium 257mg

# Zesty Ranch Fish Fillets

Prep Time: 10 minutes; Cook time: 13 minutes; Serves: 4

## Ingredients:

¾ cup finely crushed cornflakes or panko breadcrumbs
3 tbsp dry ranch-style dressing mix
1 tsp fresh lemon zest
2 ½ tbsp olive oil
2 eggs, beaten
4 white fish fillets
Lemon wedges to garnish

## Instructions:

1. Insert the dripping pan in the bottom part of the air fryer and preheat the oven at Air Fry mode at 400 F for 2 to 3 minutes.
2. Mix the cornflakes, dressing mix, lemon zest, and oil on a shallow plate and then pour the eggs on another.
3. Working in two batches, dip the fish into the egg, drip off excess egg, and coat well in the cornflakes mixture on both sides.
4. Place the fish on the cooking tray and fix the tray on the middle rack of the oven. Close the oven and set the timer for 13 minutes, and cook until the fish is golden brown and the fish flaky within.
5. Transfer to a serving plate and serve with the lemon wedges.

## Nutritional Facts Per Serving

Calories 409, Total Fat 23.84g, Total Carbs 3.79g, Fiber 0.5g, Protein 42.55g, Sugar 1.41g, Sodium 322mg

# Dill Fish Chops

Prep Time: 10 minutes; Cook time: 11 minutes; Serves: 4

**Ingredients:**

4 (5 oz) cod fillets, cut into 2-inch cubes
½ cup tapioca starch
2 eggs
1 cup almond flour
1 ½ dried fish seasoning
1 ½ dried dill
Salt and black pepper to taste
½ tsp mustard powder
Olive oil for greasing

**Instructions:**

1. Insert the dripping pan in the bottom part of the air fryer and preheat the oven at Air Fry mode at 390 F for 2 to 3 minutes.
2. Pour the tapioca starch on a shallow plate, beat the eggs in a medium bowl, and mix the almond flour, fish seasoning, dill, salt, black pepper, and mustard powder on another plate.
3. Lightly coat the fish cubes in the starch, then dip in the eggs, and coat generously in the mustard mixture until well coated on all sides.
4. Spray the coated fish with a little olive oil and put it in the rotisserie basket. Fit the basket in the oven using the rotisserie ling and close the oven. Set the timer for 11 minutes and cook until the fish is golden brown on the outside.
5. Transfer the crusted fish onto serving plates and serve warm with your favorite sauce.

**Nutritional Facts Per Serving**

Calories 206, Total Fat 4.02g, Total Carbs 18.18g, Fiber 0.4g, Protein 22.79g, Sugar 1.31g, Sodium 398mg

# Easy Fish Sticks with Chili Ketchup Sauce

Prep Time: 10 minutes; Cook time: 12 minutes; Serves: 4

## Ingredients:

8 fish sticks, store bought
½ cup tomato ketchup
1 tbsp Sriracha sauce
1 tbsp chopped fresh parsley to garnish
Sliced pickles for serving

## Instructions:

1. Insert the dripping pan in the bottom part of the air fryer and preheat the oven at Air Fry mode at 390 F for 2 to 3 minutes.
2. Arrange the fish sticks on the cooking tray and fit onto the middle rack of the oven. Close and set the timer for 12 minutes and cook until the fish sticks are golden brown and crispy.
3. Meanwhile, in a small bowl, mix the tomato ketchup, Sriracha sauce, and parsley until well combined and set aside for serving.
4. When the fish is ready, transfer onto serving plates and serve warm with the sauce and pickles.

## Nutritional Facts Per Serving

Calories 341, Total Fat 2.53g, Total Carbs 1.13g, Fiber 0.4g, Protein 73.57g, Sugar 0.69g, Sodium 568mg

# Chapter 6 Beef, Lamb & Pork

## Lunch Steak with Asparagus

Prep Time: 10 minutes + 2 hours or more marinating; Cook time: 13 minutes; Serves: 4

**Ingredients:**
4 boneless chuck eye sirloin steaks
1 to 2 tbsp favorite steak marinade
1 lb. asparagus, hard stems removed
1 tbsp olive oil
Salt to taste

**Instructions:**
1. Season the steaks on both sides with the marinade, wrap the meat in plastic wrap, and allow marinating in the refrigerator for at least 2 hours.
2. When the steak is ready, insert the dripping pan at the bottom of the oven, close the device, and preheat at Bake mode at 350 F for 2 to 3 minutes.
3. Season the asparagus with some olive oil and salt, and spread half of the vegetables on the cooking tray. Unwrap and place two steaks on the asparagus, and slide the tray onto the middle rack of the oven.
4. Close the device, set the timer for 13 minutes, and press Start. Cook until the timer reads to the end while turning the vegetables and beef halfway.
5. When ready, transfer the food onto serving plates and cook the remaining asparagus and meat in the same manner.
6. Enjoy the food warm.

**Nutrition Facts Per Serving**
Calories 609, Total Fat 28.49g, Total Carbs 5.1g, Fiber 2.4g, Protein 84.9g, Sugar 2.77g, Sodium 364mg

# Honey Balsamic Steak Bites

Prep Time: 10 minutes + 2 hours or more marinating; Cook time: 10 minutes; Serves: 4

## Ingredients:

2 tbsp olive oil
¼ cup balsamic vinegar
½ tsp red chili flakes
1 tbsp freshly crushed garlic
2 tsp dried rosemary
1/3 cup honey
3 tbs soy sauce
Salt and black pepper to taste
2 lbs. top sirloin steak, cut into 1-inch cubes
1 tbsp chopped fresh scallions for garnishing

## Instructions:

1. In a medium bowl, mix 1 tbsp of the olive oil with the remaining ingredients except for the meat until well combined.
2. Add the beef cubes and mix well with the marinade. Cover the bowl with a plastic wrap and allow marinating in the refrigerator for at least 2 hours.
3. After marinating, insert the dripping pan at the bottom of the air fryer and preheat the oven at Air Fry mode at 400 F for 2 to 3 minutes.
4. Grease the rotisserie basket with the remaining olive oil and using a tongs, transfer the meat bites to the basket while making sure to shake off as much marinade from the meat to reduce mess. Also, make sure the meat bites are spread across the basket well.
5. Place the basket in the oven using the rotisserie lift, close the oven, set the timer for 10 minutes, and press Start. Cook until the timer reads to the end or until the meat is light brown and cook within.
6. Transfer the meat to serving plates and garnish with the scallions.
7. Serve warm.

## Nutrition Facts Per Serving

Calories 632, Total Fat 34.26g, Total Carbs 30.86g, Fiber 0.7, Protein 48.36g, Sugar 28.32g, Sodium 317mg

# Pop's Steak and Potato Mix

Prep Time: 10 minutes; Cook time: 15 or 18 minutes; Serves: 4

**Ingredients:**

1 lb. chuck steak, cut into ½ -inch cubes and patted dry

½ lb. baby potatoes, washed and cut into ½ -inch pieces

2 tbsp olive oil

½ tsp garlic powder

Salt and black pepper to taste

1 tsp Worcestershire sauce

1 tbsp melted butter for topping

1 tsp red chili flakes for topping

2 tbsp chopped fresh parsley to garnish

**Instructions:**

1. Insert the dripping pan at the bottom of the air fryer and preheat the oven at Roast mode at 400 F for 2 to 3 minutes.
2. In a large bowl, add and mix the meat, potatoes, olive oil, garlic powder, salt, black pepper, and Worcestershire sauce until the meat and potatoes are well coated with the seasoning.
3. Spoon the mixture into the rotisserie basket and fit the basket into the oven using the rotisserie lings.
4. Close the oven, set the timer for 15 or 18 minutes (depending on your desired doneness), and press Start. Cook until the timer reads to the end.
5. When ready, transfer the food to serving plates. Drizzle the butter on top and garnish with the parsley and chili flakes.
6. Serve immediately.

**Nutrition Facts Per Serving**

Calories 290, Total Fat 14.73g, Total Carbs 14.99g, Fiber 2g, Protein 26.08g, Sugar 3.67g, Sodium 123mg

# Coffee Spiced Rib Eye Steak

Prep Time: 30 minutes; Cook time: 14 minutes; Serves: 4

## Ingredients:

1 tsp brown sugar
¼ tsp chipotle powder
1/8 tsp coriander powder
¼ tsp paprika
½ tsp ground coffee
½ tsp black pepper
¼ tsp chili powder
1/8 tsp cocoa powder
1 ½ tsp salt
¼ tsp garlic powder
¼ tsp onion powder
1 lb. ribeye steak

## Instructions:

1. Insert the dripping pan at the bottom of the air fryer and preheat the oven at Roast mode at 390 F for 2 to 3 minutes.
2. In a small bowl, mix all the ingredients except for the meat and then, season the meat well and on both sides with the spice mix. Allow sitting at room temperature for 20 minutes to marinate.
3. After, place the meat on the cooking tray, insert the tray on the middle rack of the oven, and close the device.
4. Set the timer for 9 minutes and press Start. Cook the meat undisturbed until the timer reads to the end.
5. When ready, transfer the meat onto a clean, flat surface and allow resting for 5 minutes before slicing.
6. Serve warm afterwards.

## Nutrition Facts Per Serving

Calories 218, Total Fat 12.99g, Total Carbs 3.31g, Fiber 0.3g, Protein 22.21g, Sugar 0.66g, Sodium 977mg

# Herb Crusted Roast

Prep Time: 5 minutes + 20 minutes marinating; Cook time: 90 minutes; Serves: 4

**Ingredients:**

2 tsp garlic powder

2 tsp onion powder

2 tsp dried basil

2 tsp dried parsley

2 tsp dried thyme

½ tbsp salt

1 tsp black pepper

2 lbs. beef roast

1 tbsp olive oil

**Instructions:**

1. Insert the dripping pan at the bottom of the air fryer and preheat the oven at Roast mode at 390 F for 2 to 3 minutes.
2. In a small bowl, mix all the ingredients except for the meat and olive oil. Rub the herb mixture all around the meat making sure to press the herb mix onto the meat to stick. Allow marinating for 20 minutes at room temperature.
3. Grease the cooking tray with the olive oil and sit the roast on top. Slide the cooking pan onto the middle rack of the oven, and close the air fryer.
4. Set the timer for 15 minutes and press Start.
5. After 15 minutes, turn the roast over, close the oven, and reduce the temperature to 360 F. Cook at a set time of 60 minutes in the same mode or until the meat is done.
6. Transfer the meat to clean, flat surface when ready, allow sitting for 15 minutes, slice, and serve afterwards.

**Nutrition Facts Per Serving**

Calories 457, Total Fat 22.64g, Total Carbs 2.84g, Fiber 0.7g, Protein 61.02g, Sugar 0.13g, Sodium 1056mg

# Sesame BBQ Beef

Prep Time: 10 minutes; Cook time: 14 minutes; Serves: 4

## Ingredients:
Sesame oil for spraying
1 lb. flank steak, thinly sliced
¼ cup corn starch
½ cup soy sauce
½ cup brown sugar
2 tbsp plain vinegar
1 clove garlic, crushed
1 tbsp hot chili sauce
1 tsp fresh ginger puree
½ tsp sesame seeds
1 tbsp cornstarch
1 tbsp water

## Instructions:
1. Insert the dripping pan at the bottom of the air fryer and preheat the oven at Bake mode at 390 F for 2 to 3 minutes. Also, lightly brush the rotisserie basket with some sesame oil.
2. In a medium bowl, mix the beef with the corn starch and add the meat to the rotisserie basket. Spray lightly with some sesame oil.
3. Fit the basket into the oven using the rotisserie lings, close the air fryer, set the timer for 10 minutes, and press Start. Cook until the timer reads to the end.
4. Meanwhile, in a medium bowl, mix the remaining ingredients, and when the meat is ready, add the pieces to the mixture in the bowl and combine well.
5. Transfer the mixture to a 6-inch casserole bowl, place the bowl on the cooking tray, and slide the tray onto the middle rack of the oven.
6. Close the oven, set the time for 5 minutes and Press Start. Cook until the sauce is syrupy.
7. Remove the dish from the oven, stir well, and allow sitting for 2 to 3 minutes before serving.

**Nutrition Facts Per Serving**
Calories 408, Total Fat 12.16g, Total Carbs 45.72g, Fiber 1.7g, Protein 27.82g, Sugar 33.39g, Sodium 611mg

# BBQ Beef Meatballs

Prep Time: 12 minutes; Cook time: 15 minutes; Serves: 4

**Ingredients:**
Olive oil for brushing
1 lb. ground beef
½ cup breadcrumbs
½ cup chopped white onions
2 garlic cloves, minced
1 egg, beaten
¼ cup shredded Monterey Jack cheese
1 tsp Worcestershire sauce
1 tsp your favorite steak seasoning
Salt and black pepper to taste
½ cup sugar-free BBQ Sauce

**Instructions:**
1. Insert the dripping pan at the bottom of the air fryer and preheat the oven at Air Fry mode at 370 F for 2 to 3 minutes. Also, lightly brush the cooking tray with some olive oil and set aside.
2. In a medium bowl, mix the beef, breadcrumbs, onions, garlic, egg, Monterey Jack cheese, Worcestershire sauce, steak seasoning, salt, and black pepper. Form 2-inch size meatballs from the mixture, arrange on the cooking tray, and brush with the BBQ sauce.
3. Slide the cooking tray onto the middle rack of the air fryer and close the oven.
4. Set the timer for 15 minutes, and press Start. Cook the meatballs until the timer reads to the end while turning halfway.
5. When ready, transfer to serving plates and serve warm.

**Nutrition Facts Per Serving**
Calories 344, Total Fat 18.57g, Total Carbs 6.75g, Fiber 0.7g, Protein 35.29g, Sugar 1.32g, Sodium 269mg

# Sweet Italian Meatloaf

Prep Time: 10 minutes; Cook time: 35 minutes; Serves: 4

## Ingredients:

2 tsp canola oil
½ small onion, chopped
1 lb. ground beef
1 tsp Worcestershire sauce
1 tsp Italian seasoning
½ tsp salt
¼ tsp black pepper
½ tsp garlic powder
¼ cup panko breadcrumbs
2 tbsp ketchup, divided
1 egg, lightly beaten
1 tbsp yellow mustard

## Instructions:

1. Insert the dripping pan at the bottom of the air fryer and preheat the oven at Bake mode at 370 F for 2 to 3 minutes. Also, lightly brush the inner parts of a 6-inch loaf or cake pan (safe for the air fryer) with canola oil and set aside.
2. In a medium bowl, mix the remaining ingredients except for 1 tbsp of ketchup and spoon the mixture into the loaf pan while making sure to press to fit well.
3. Slide the cooking tray onto the middle rack of the oven, place the loaf pan on top, and close the oven. Set the timer to 15 minutes and press Start. Cook the food until the timer reads to the end.
4. After, remove the loaf pan from the oven and spread the remaining ketchup on top. Return the pan to the oven and cook further for 8 to 10 minutes.
5. When ready, remove the pan, allow the meatloaf to rest for 5 to 10 minutes before slicing and serving.

## Nutrition Facts Per Serving

Calories 311, Total Fat 17.08g, Total Carbs 4.91g, Fiber 0.5g, Protein 32.52g, Sugar 2.83g, Sodium 626mg

# Bell Pepper and Beef Stir Fry

Prep Time: 10 minutes + 30 minutes marinating; Cook time: 10 minutes; Serves: 4

**Ingredients:**

1 lb. beef sirloin, cut into 2 inch strips

1 large red bell pepper, deseeded and cut into strips

1 large green bell pepper, deseeded and cut into strips

1 large yellow bell pepper, deseeded and cut into strips

1 small yellow onion, sliced

1 small red onion, sliced

1 tbsp soy sauce

¼ cup of hoisin sauce

1 tsp fresh ginger paste

2 garlic cloves, minced

1 tsp sesame oil

2 tbsp water

**Instructions:**

1. Insert the dripping pan at the bottom of the air fryer and preheat the oven at Air Fry mode at 360 F for 2 to 3 minutes.
2. In a bowl, add the meat, bell pepper, and onions. In a small bowl, mix the soy sauce, hoisin sauce, ginger paste, garlic, sesame oil, and water. Pour the mixture over the vegetables and meat, and combine well. Set aside to marinate for at least 30 minutes.
3. After, using a slotted spoon, transfer the meat and vegetables onto the cooking tray while making sure to drain off as much of the marinade as possible.
4. Slide the tray onto the middle rack of the oven, set the timer for 5 minutes, and press Start.
5. When the timer is done, open the oven, stir the food, and repeat cooking for 5 more minutes in the same setting.
6. Transfer to serving plates when ready and serve.

**Nutrition Facts Per Serving**

Calories 301, Total Fat 15.12g, Total Carbs 15.09g, Fiber 1.7g, Protein 25.43g, Sugar 8.36g, Sodium 383mg

# Mushroom and Beef Meatballs

Prep Time: 10 minutes; Cook time: 10 minutes; Serves: 4

**Ingredients:**
1 lb. ground beef
¼ cup chopped cremini mushrooms
¼ cup chopped yellow onion
½ cup panko breadcrumbs
1/8 cup chopped fresh parsley
Salt and black pepper to taste
1 tbsp olive oil

**Instructions:**
1. Insert the dripping pan at the bottom of the air fryer and preheat the oven at Air Fry mode at 370 F for 2 to 3 minutes. Also, lightly brush the cooking tray with some olive oil and set aside.
2. In a medium bowl, mix all the ingredients and form 2-inch size meatballs from the mixture, arrange on the cooking tray, and brush with a little oil.
3. Slide the cooking tray onto the middle rack of the air fryer and close the oven. Set the timer for 15 minutes, and press Start. Cook the meatballs until the timer reads to the end while turning halfway.
4. When ready, transfer to serving plates and serve warm.

**Nutrition Facts Per Serving**
Calories 286, Total Fat 16.61g, Total Carbs 1.81g, Fiber 0.4g, Protein 30.71g, Sugar 0.95g, Sodium 72mg

# Lamb Roast with Vegetables

Prep Time: 10 minutes; Cook time: 45 minutes; Serves: 4

**Ingredients:**

2 tbsp olive oil

2 lbs. boneless leg of lamb (tied into a roast)

Salt and black pepper to taste

3 garlic cloves, minced

1 tsp chopped fresh rosemary leaves

1 lb. mixed roots vegetables, peeled and cut into chunks

**Instructions:**

1. Insert the dripping pan at the bottom of the air fryer and preheat the oven at Roast mode at 375 F for 2 to 3 minutes. Also, lightly brush an 8-inch casserole dish with some olive oil and set aside.
2. Pat the lamb dry on all sides, brush with the remaining olive oil, season well with salt, black pepper, and set aside.
3. In a small bowl, mix the garlic, rosemary, and rub the mixture all around the lamb.
4. Season the vegetables with some olive oil, salt, and spread in the bottom of the casserole dish. Sit the lamb on top.
5. Slide the cooking tray upside down onto the middle rack of the oven and place the casserole dish on top.
6. Close the oven, set the time for 40 minutes, and press Start. Cook until the vegetables read to the end while the vegetables and meat halfway.
7. When the food is ready, transfer the meat to a flat surface to cool for 5 minutes before slicing.
8. Serve the meat warm with the vegetables.

**Nutrition Facts Per Serving**

Calories 462, Total Fat 20.18g, Total Carbs 17.12g, Fiber 4.8g, Protein 50.6g, Sugar 0.6g, Sodium 236mg

# Leg of Lamb with Tomatoes, Mint, and Olives

Prep Time: 10 minutes; Cook time: 45 minutes; Serves: 4

## Ingredients:

1 tbsp olive oil
2 lbs. leg of lamb
½ tsp coriander powder
Salt and black pepper to taste
½ tsp cloves powder
1 tbsp vegetable oil
1 onion, thinly sliced
1 garlic clove, minced
1 small can whole tomatoes
¼ cup black olives, pitted & halved
3 tbsp chopped fresh mint
1 tbsp plain vinegar

## Instructions:

1. Heat the olive oil in a large skillet over medium heat. In a small bowl, quickly mix the coriander powder, salt, black pepper, cloves powder, and season the lamb on both sides with the spice mix. Sear the lamb on both sides in the oil until golden brown, 10 minutes.
2. Meanwhile, heat the vegetable oil in a medium skillet over medium heat and sauté the onion and garlic until fragrant and softened, 3 minutes. Stir in the tomatoes and olives until slightly softened, 5 minutes. Season with salt, black pepper, and mix in the mint and vinegar.
3. Insert the dripping pan at the bottom of the air fryer and preheat the oven at Roast mode at 350 F for 2 to 3 minutes.
4. Spoon the sauce into an 8-inch casserole dish and sit the leg of lamb in the sauce. Baste with some of the sauce.
5. Fix the cooking tray upside down on the middle rack of the oven, sit the dish on top, and close the oven.
6. Set the time for 20 minutes, and press Start. Cook until the lamb reaches an internal temperature of 130 to 135 F. Meanwhile, check the food every 10 minutes and if the sauce is too dry, add in a little water. Also, flip the meat halfway.
7. When ready, remove the dish from the oven, allow sitting for 5 minutes, and serve afterwards.

## Nutrition Facts Per Serving

Calories 631, Total Fat 32.66g, Total Carbs 3.19g, Fiber 0.8g, Protein 76.6g, Sugar 1.31g, Sodium 277mg

# Roast Rack of Lamb with Rosemary

Prep Time: 5 minutes; Cook time: 35 minutes; Serves: 4

## Ingredients:

2 x 8-boned French lamb racks
2 heaped tsp finely chopped fresh rosemary
Salt to taste
2 tbsp olive oil

## Instructions:

1. Insert the dripping pan at the bottom of the air fryer and preheat the oven at Roast mode at 400 F for 2 to 3 minutes.
2. Season the lamb racks on both sides with the rosemary, salt, and brush with the olive oil.
3. Place the lamb rack on the cooking tray and fit onto the middle rack of the oven.
4. Close the oven, set the timer for 20 or 25 minutes depending on your desired doneness, and press Start. Cook until the timer reads to the end while flipping halfway.
5. Open the oven, remove the food, and allow sitting for 10 minutes.
6. Slice through the racks and serve the meat warm.

## Nutrition Facts Per Serving

Calories 60, Total Fat 6.77g, Total Carbs 0.07g, Fiber 0g, Protein 0.01g, Sugar 0g, Sodium 0mg

# Herb Crusted Lamb Loins

Prep Time: 10 minutes; Cook time: 20 minutes; Serves: 2

## Ingredients:

3 tbsp olive oil
2 tsp chopped fresh rosemary
½ cup chopped scallions
2 garlic cloves, minced
Salt and black pepper to taste
1 tbsp chopped fresh mint leaves
1 tbsp chopped fresh parsley
2 (12 oz) boneless single lamb loin roasts, trimmed
½ cup panko breadcrumbs
1 tbsp Dijon mustard
2 tsp maple syrup

## Instructions:

1. Heat 1 tbsp olive oil in small skillet and sauté the rosemary, scallions, and garlic until softened, 30 seconds. Season with salt, black pepper, and mix in the mint and parsley. Turn the heat off and allow the herbs wilt. Set aside to cool.
2. Heat the remaining olive oil in a medium skillet, season the lamb loins with salt, black pepper, and sear in the oil on both sides until golden brown. Turn the heat off.
3. Mix the breadcrumbs, mustard, and maple syrup into the herb mixture. Cover the meat pieces on all sides with the breadcrumbs mix and place on the cooking tray (lightly greased with some olive oil).
4. Insert the dripping pan at the bottom of the air fryer and preheat the oven at Roast mode at 375 F for 2 to 3 minutes.
5. Slide the cooking tray onto the middle rack of the oven and close. Set the timer for 15 minutes and press Start.
6. When ready, remove the meat from the oven, allow sitting for 5 minutes, slice, and serve warm afterwards.

## Nutrition Facts Per Serving

Calories 112, Total Fat 10.34g, Total Carbs 5.07g, Fiber 0.8g, Protein 0.75g, Sugar 0.02g, Sodium 47mg

# Roasted Greek Lamb with Potatoes and Bell Peppers

Prep Time: 15 minutes + 2 hours marinating; Cook time: 25 minutes; Serves: 4

## Ingredients:

1 ½ lbs. lean lamb, cut into bite-size chunks
3 tbsp olive oil
Salt and black pepper to taste
4 bay leaves, cut into halves
1 ½ tsp dried oregano
1 lemon, juiced
2 garlic cloves, minced
4 large potatoes, peeled, cut into 1-inch cubes, and steamed
1 large red bell pepper, deseeded and cut into 1-inch pieces
1 tbsp light brown sugar

## Instructions:

1. In a large bowl, mix the lamb chunks, 2 tbsp of the olive oil, salt, black pepper, bay leaves, oregano, lemon juice, and garlic until well combined. Cover the bowl with a plastic wrap and marinate in the refrigerator for 1 to 2 hours.
2. After the meat marinates, insert the dripping pan at the bottom of the air fryer and preheat the oven at Roast mode at 375 F for 2 to 3 minutes.
3. In a medium bowl, mix the potatoes, bell pepper, brown sugar, remaining olive oil, and lamb. Pour the mixture into an 8-inch cake pan (safe for the oven).
4. Slide the cooking tray upside down onto the middle rack of the oven, place the dish on top, and close the oven.
5. Set the timer for 20 to 25 minutes depending on your desired doneness, and press Start. Cook until the timer reads to the end while stirring the food halfway.
6. Remove the dish from the oven when ready and serve warm.

## Nutrition Facts Per Serving

Calories 824, Total Fat 39.17g, Total Carbs 68.18g, Fiber 8.7g, Protein 49.78g, Sugar 4.36g, Sodium 154mg

# Maple Ginger Pork Tenderloin

Prep Time: 10 minutes + 2 hours marinating; Cook time: 30 minutes; Serves: 4

**Ingredients:**

1 ½ tbsp fresh grated ginger

7 tbsp maple syrup

2 freshly squeezed lemon juice

2 tsp pressed garlic

2 ½ tbsp soy sauce

Salt and black pepper to taste

A pinch cayenne pepper

1 lb. pork tenderloin, excess fat trimmed

Olive oil for brushing

2 tbsp chopped fresh chives for garnishing

**Instructions:**

1. In a medium bowl, mix all the ingredients up to the pork and pour into a large zipper bag. Add the pork, seal the bag, and rub the marinade well onto the meat. Allow marinating in the refrigerator for 2 hours.
2. Once done marinating, heat 1 tbsp of the olive oil in a large skillet, remove the pork from marinade, and sear in the oil on both sides until golden brown, 3 to 4 minutes per side.
3. Meanwhile, insert the dripping pan onto the bottom part of the oven and preheat at Roast mode at 400 F for 2 to 3 minutes.
4. When the pork is ready, transfer to the cooking tray and brush all around with a little more olive oil. Slide the cooking tray onto the middle rack of the oven and close.
5. Set the timer to 10 to 15 minutes depending on your desired doneness, and press Start.
6. After the cooking time ends, slide out the tray, baste the meat with the leftover marinade, turn the meat over, and cook further for 1 to 2 minutes in the same setting or until golden brown.
7. Remove the meat from the oven and cover with foil and allow resting for 5 minutes before slicing.
8. Garnish with the chives and serve warm.

**Nutrition Facts Per Serving**

Calories 301, Total Fat 5.94g, Total Carbs 30.65g, Fiber 0.7g, Protein 31.11g, Sugar 24.91g, Sodium 222mg

# Honey Glazed Pork Shoulder

Prep Time: 12 minutes + 2 hour marinating; Cook time: 67 minutes; Serves: 4

## Ingredients:

1 tsp fennel seeds, crushed

Salt to taste

¼ cup brown sugar

1 tsp whole black peppercorns, crushed

6 lbs. skinless bone-in pork shoulder

¼ cup + 1 tbsp apple cider vinegar

¼ cup honey

½ tsp black pepper

## Instructions:

1. In a small bowl, mix the fennel seeds, salt, brown sugar, and peppercorns. Rub the spice mix on both sides of the pork, cover with plastic wrap, and set aside to marinate for at least 2 hours.
2. When done marinating, preheat the oven at Bake mode at 400 F for 2 to 3 minutes.
3. Replace the pork cover with foil (meanwhile shaking off some of the rub before wrapping), place on the cooking tray and slide the tray onto the middle rack of the air fryer oven. Also, fill the dripping pan with water, carefully place on the bottom of the oven and close.
4. Set the timer for 1 hour, and cook until the timer reads to the end. If the meat isn't tender, cook further for 30 to 45 minutes.
5. Meanwhile, in a small bowl, whisk the apple cider vinegar, honey, and black pepper to make the glaze. Set aside.
6. When the meat is ready, remove the cooking tray, unwrap the pork, brush the top with the glaze, and return the meat to the oven.
7. Cook further in the same mode but for 12 minutes or until golden brown.
8. Transfer the meat to a clean, flat surface, allow sitting for 10 minutes before slicing.
9. Serve warm.

## Nutrition Facts Per Serving

Calories 991, Total Fat 23.28g, Total Carbs 33.27g, Fiber 0.4g, Protein 153.62g, Sugar 32.31g, Sodium 374mg

# Memphis Style Pork Ribs

Prep Time: 10 minutes; Cook time: 38 minutes; Serves: 4

**Ingredients:**

1 tsp garlic powder

1 tsp onion powder

1 tbsp salt

½ tsp black pepper

1 tsp beef seasoning

½ tsp mustard powder

1 tbsp dark brown sugar

1 tbsp sweet paprika

2 ¼ lbs. pork spareribs, individually cut

**Instructions:**

1. Insert the dripping pan onto the bottom part of the oven and preheat at Air Fry mode at 350 F for 2 to 3 minutes.
2. In a small bowl, mix all the ingredients up to the spare ribs and them and rub the spice mixture on all sides of each rib.
3. Arrange the 4 to 6 ribs on the cooking tray, slide the tray onto the middle rack of the oven, and close the oven.
4. Set the timer for 35 minutes, and press Start. Cook until the ribs are golden brown and tender within while flipping every halfway.
5. Transfer to a plate when ready and allow cooling for 2 to 3 minutes before serving.

**Nutrition Facts Per Serving**

Calories 618, Total Fat 35.7g, Total Carbs 2.23g, Fiber 0.9g, Protein 67.75g, Sugar 0.24g, Sodium 1899mg

# Thyme Roasted Pork Chops

Prep Time: 10 minutes; Cook time: 25 minutes; Serves: 4

**Ingredients:**

4 pork chops bone-in, loin, about 3/4-inch thickness
1 tbsp olive oil
¼ tsp garlic powder
¼ tsp dried thyme
Salt and black pepper to taste

**Instructions:**

1. Insert the dripping pan onto the bottom part of the oven and preheat at Roast mode at 400 F for 2 to 3 minutes.
2. Brush the meat on both sides with olive oil and season with the garlic powder, thyme, salt, and black pepper. Place two chops on the cooking tray, slide the tray onto the middle rack of oven and close.
3. Set the timer to 20 or 25 minutes depending on your desired doneness and press Start. Cook until the timer ends or until the meat is golden brown and tender within while flipping halfway.
4. Transfer to serving plates and cook the other two chops in the same manner.
5. Serve the chops immediately with buttered vegetables.

**Nutrition Facts Per Serving**

Calories 363, Total Fat 20.76g, Total Carbs 1.22g, Fiber 0.2g, Protein 40.47g, Sugar 0.58g, Sodium 87mg

# Bake Barbecued Pork Chops

Prep Time: 10 minutes; Cook time: 52 minutes; Serves: 4

**Ingredients:**

4 bone-in pork chops, thick cut
Salt and black pepper to taste
½ tsp garlic powder
¼ tsp cayenne pepper
¼ cup brown sugar
2 tbsp honey
1 cup ketchup
½ cup hot sauce
1 tsp apple cider vinegar
½ tsp paprika
1 tbsp Worcestershire sauce
1 tbsp yellow mustard
¼ tsp celery salt

**Instructions:**

1. Preheat the oven at Bake mode at 350 F for 2 to 3 minutes and lightly grease an 8-inch baking dish (safe for the air fryer) with olive oil. Set aside.
2. Season the pork chops with salt, black pepper, and lay in the baking dish.
3. In a small bowl, mix the remaining ingredients and pour the mixture all over the meat while lifting the meat a little to have some of the spice mix go under the chops. Cover the dish with foil.
4. Slide the cooking tray upside down on the middle rack of the oven, place the baking dish on top and close the air fryer.
5. Set the timer for 45 or 50 minutes, and press Start. Cook until the timer reads to the end while opening the dish and turning the meat.
6. Once the timer ends, take off the foil, set the air fryer in Broil mode and press Start to brown the top of the pork.
7. When ready, remove the dish from the oven, allow sitting for 2 minutes and serve afterwards.

**Nutrition Facts Per Serving**

Calories 489, Total Fat 17.75g, Total Carbs 41.74g, Fiber 0.8g, Protein 41.52g, Sugar 0.02g, Sodium 1482mg

# Chapter 7 Poultry

## Beer Buffalo Wings

Prep Time: 10 minutes + 30 minutes marinating; Cook time: 35 minutes; Serves: 4

**Ingredients:**

1 tbsp brown sugar
2 tsp salt
1 (12 oz) can regular or non-alcoholic beer
2 lbs. chicken wings
1 tbsp paprika
½ tsp garlic powder
½ tsp onion powder
½ tsp black pepper
¼ cup butter, melted
¼ cup hot sauce

**Instructions:**

1. In a large bowl, mix the beer, brown sugar, and salt until well combined and mix in the wings until well coated with the sauce. Cover the bowl with plastic wrap and allow sitting in the refrigerator for 30 minutes to brine.
2. After 30 minutes, preheat the air fryer at Bake mode at 350 F for 2 to 3 minutes.
3. Meanwhile, in a large zipper bag, mix the paprika, garlic powder, onion powder, and black pepper. Remove the chicken from the fridge and brine, and add to the spice mix. Close the bag and work the spice well onto the chicken.
4. Wrap the cooking tray with foil and arrange half of the chicken on top.
5. In a small bowl, mix the butter with the hot sauce and pour half of the mixture all over the chicken. Slide the cooking tray onto the middle rack of the air fryer and close the lid.
6. Set the timer to 30 or 35 minutes and cook until the chicken is tender.
7. Transfer the chicken to a serving platter and make the remaining chicken in the same manner.
8. Serve warm.

**Nutrition Facts Per Serving**

Calories 443, Total Fat 19.84g, Total Carbs 7.1g, Fiber 0.8g, Protein 50.81g, Sugar 2.35g, Sodium 1824mg

# Simple Oven-Grilled Breasts

Prep Time: 10 minutes; Cook time: 18 minutes; Serves: 4

## Ingredients:

4 chicken breasts, skinless and boneless
½ cup olive oil
3 tbsp brown sugar
3 tbsp soy sauce
1 ½ fresh lemon zest
1 tbsp chopped fresh parsley + more for garnishing
1 tbsp chopped fresh thyme
Salt and black pepper to taste
2 garlic cloves, minced

## Instructions:

1. Place the chicken in a medium bowl. In another bowl, mix the remaining ingredients and pour the mixture all over the chicken. Turn the meat in the sauce to be well coated, cover the bowl with a plastic wrap, and marinate in the refrigerator for at least 1 hour.
2. After marinate, insert the dripping pan onto the bottom part of the air fryer and preheat at Bake mode at 320 F for 2 to 3 minutes.
3. Remove the chicken onto the cooking tray, slide the tray onto the middle rack of the oven and close the lid.
4. Set the timer for 16 minutes, and press Start. Cook until the timer reads to the end while flipping halfway.
5. After cooking, reset the device to Broil mode, set the time to 1 to 2 minutes, and press Start. Cook until the chicken is golden brown on top.
6. Transfer the chicken to serving plates and serve warm.

## Nutrition Facts Per Serving

Calories 807, Total Fat 56.08g, Total Carbs 11.97g, Fiber 0.6g, Protein 61.76g, Sugar 0.08g, Sodium 366mg

# Chicken Veggie Merry

Prep Time: 10 minutes; Cook time: 21 minutes; Serves: 4

**Ingredients:**

4 chicken breasts, skinless and boneless

Salt and black pepper to taste

2 tbsp olive oil

1 extra large red bell pepper, deseeded and cut into small chunks

1 medium sweet onion, peeled and cut into wedges

3 tbsp diced green chili pepper

5 garlic cloves, minced

2 tsp cumin powder

1 (15 oz) can black beans, drained and rinsed

1 cup frozen corn

2 tbsp chopped fresh scallions

1 tbsp chopped fresh parsley

**Instructions:**

1. Cut the chicken into 1-inch cubes and season with salt and black pepper.
2. Heat the olive oil in a medium skillet and sear the chicken on both sides until golden brown, 3 minutes. Transfer the chicken to an 8-inch glass casserole dish.
3. Add the bell pepper, onion, green chili, garlic, and cumin to the skillet, and cook for 1 to 2 minutes to release fragrance. Add this combination, black beans, and corn to the chicken. Season with a little more salt, black pepper, and mix well.
4. Preheat the air fryer at Bake mode at 340 F for 2 to 3 minutes.
5. Slide the cooking tray onto the middle rack of the oven, place the casserole dish on top, and close the oven.
6. Set the timer for 16 minutes and press Start. Cook until the chicken is tender and the vegetables soften.
7. Remove the dish after and mix in the scallions and parsley. Serve afterwards.

**Nutrition Facts Per Serving**

Calories 677, Total Fat 34.95g, Total Carbs 24.78g, Fiber 4g, Protein 64.42g, Sugar 8.33g, Sodium 207mg

# Mozzarella Chicken

Prep Time: 10 minutes; Cook time: 22 minutes; Serves: 4

**Ingredients:**
1 tbsp olive oil
4 chicken breasts, boneless and skinless
½ tsp onion powder
Salt and black pepper to taste
1 tbsp Italian seasoning
1 tsp paprika
1 medium white onion, chopped
4 garlic cloves, minced
2 tbsp tomato paste
¼ tsp red chili flakes
1 red roasted bell pepper
1 (15 oz) Passata
¾ cup shredded mozzarella cheese
1 tbsp chopped fresh parsley

**Instructions:**
1. Heat the olive oil in a medium pot, season the chicken with the onion powder, salt, black pepper, Italian seasoning, paprika, and sear on both sides in the oil until golden brown, 5 minutes. Transfer to a plate and set aside.
2. Sauté the onion and garlic in the skillet until softened and fragrant, and mix in the tomato paste, red chili flakes, bell pepper, and Passata. Cover the lid and simmer until the sauce thickens, 10 minutes. Season with salt and black pepper.
3. When the sauce is near done, insert the dripping pan into the air fryer and preheat Broil mode at 340 F for 2 to 3 minutes.
4. Pour the sauce into a 9-inch square, glass-baking dish, lay each chicken breast in the sauce, and spread the mozzarella cheese on top.
5. Slide the cooking tray onto the middle rack of the oven, place the dish on top, and close the oven.
6. Set the timer to 1 to 2 minutes, and press Start. Cook until the cheese browns and is bubbly.
7. Remove the dish after, garnish the food with the parsley and serve warm.

**Nutrition Facts Per Serving**
Calories 600, Total Fat 30.45g, Total Carbs 9.94g, Fiber 2.3g, Protein 68.68g, Sugar 4.19g, Sodium 552mg

# Maple Garlic Chicken

Prep Time: 10 minutes; Cook time: 27 minutes; Serves: 4

## Ingredients:

1 tbsp olive oil
4 chicken thighs, skinless and boneless
Salt and black pepper to taste
2 tsp garlic powder
1/3 cup maple syrup
¼ cup chicken broth
6 garlic cloves, crushed
2 tbsp apple cider vinegar
1 tbsp soy sauce

## Instructions:

1. Heat the olive oil in a medium skillet, season the chicken with the salt, black pepper, garlic powder, and sear the meat in the oil on both sides until golden brown, 5 minutes. Transfer to an 8-inch glass-baking dish.
2. In a medium bowl, mix the remaining ingredients and pour the mixture over the chicken.
3. Insert the dripping pan onto the bottom of the air fryer oven and preheat at Bake mode at 340 F for 2 to 3 minutes.
4. Slide the cooking tray upside down onto the middle rack of the oven, place the dish on the tray and close the oven.
5. Set the timer for 20 minutes and press Start. Cook until the timer reads to the end or the sauce slightly thickens.
6. Turn the oven to Broil mode and brown the top of the chicken for 1 to 2 minutes.
7. When ready, dish the food and serve warm.

## Nutrition Facts Per Serving

Calories 577, Total Fat 37.26g, Total Carbs 22.77g, Fiber 0.5g, Protein 36.19g, Sugar 17.17g, Sodium 284mg

# Pancetta Wrapped Breasts

Prep Time: 10 minutes; Cook time: 23 minutes; Serves: 4

**Ingredients:**

4 chicken breasts, skinless and boneless
Salt and black pepper
1 tsp garlic powder
8–12 pancetta slices
4 tbsp melted butter
1 tbsp chopped fresh sage
A pinch red chili flakes
¼ cup dry white wine
1 tbsp chopped fresh parsley to garnish
1 lemon, cut into wedges for serving

**Instructions:**

1. Season the chicken on both sides with salt, black pepper, garlic powder, and wrap each with 2 to 3 pancetta slices making sure to tuck in the ends well.
2. In an 8-inch rectangular baking dish, mix the butter, sage, red chili flakes, white wine, and lay in the chicken.
3. Insert the dripping pan onto the bottom of the air fryer oven and preheat at Bake mode at 340 F for 2 to 3 minutes.
8. After, slide the cooking tray upside down onto the middle rack of the oven, place the dish on the tray and close the oven.
4. Set the timer for 16 minutes and press Start. Cook until the timer reads to the end.
5. Transfer the chicken to serving plates when ready, allow sitting for 1 to 2 minutes and serve afterwards.

**Nutrition Facts Per Serving**

Calories 1105, Total Fat 59.05g, Total Carbs 9.5g, Fiber 0.6g, Protein 132.88g, Sugar 7.68g, Sodium 5010mg

# Creamy Turmeric Chicken

Prep Time: 10 minutes; Cook time: 29 minutes; Serves: 4

## Ingredients:

2 tbsp butter
4 chicken thighs, boneless and skinless
Salt and black pepper to taste
1 medium yellow onion, thinly sliced
1 tsp turmeric powder
½ cup dry white wine
½ cup coconut cream
½ cup chicken broth
2 tbsp chopped fresh cilantro for garnishing

## Instructions:

1. Melt 2 tbsp of butter in medium pot, season the chicken on both sides with salt, black pepper, and sear in the butter until golden brown, 5 minutes. Transfer to a plate and set aside.
2. Sauté the onion in the pan until softened and mix in the turmeric powder, white wine, coconut cream, chicken broth, and season with salt and black pepper. Simmer for 3 to 4 minutes and pour the sauce into an 8-inch glass-baking dish. Lay the chicken in the sauce.
3. Insert the dripping pan onto the bottom of the air fryer oven and preheat at Bake mode at 340 F for 2 to 3 minutes.
4. After, slide the cooking tray upside down onto the middle rack of the oven, place the dish on the tray and close the oven.
5. Set the timer for 20 minutes and press Start. Cook until the timer reads to the end.
6. Remove the dish when ready and serve the chicken with sauce warm.

## Nutrition Facts Per Serving

Calories 671, Total Fat 53.3g, Total Carbs 4.76g, Fiber 1.1g, Protein 42.82g, Sugar 0.77g, Sodium 547mg

# Garlic Butter Chicken

Prep Time: 10 minutes; Cook time: 21 minutes; Serves: 4

**Ingredients:**

1 tbsp olive oil

4 chicken breasts, boneless and skinless

Salt and black pepper to taste

1 tsp paprika

4 tbsp melted butter

2 garlic cloves, minced

1 tsp Italian seasoning

1 tbsp chopped fresh parsley

**Instructions:**

1. Heat the olive oil in a medium skillet, season the chicken with salt, black pepper, paprika, and sear the chicken in the oil on both sides until golden brown, 5 minutes. Transfer to an 8-inch baking dish and set aside.
2. In a small bowl, mix the remaining ingredients and pour the mixture all over the chicken.
3. Insert the dripping pan onto the bottom of the air fryer oven and preheat at Bake mode at 340 F for 2 to 3 minutes.
4. After, slide the cooking tray upside down onto the middle rack of the oven, place the dish on the tray and close the oven.
5. Set the timer for 16 minutes and press Start. Cook until the timer reads to the end.
6. Remove the dish when ready and serve the chicken with sauce warm.

**Nutrition Facts Per Serving**

Calories 641, Total Fat 41.83g, Total Carbs 2.36g, Fiber 0.5g, Protein 61.05g, Sugar 0.74g, Sodium 328mg

# Lemon Roasted Chicken

Prep Time: 10 minutes; Cook time: 55 minutes; Serves: 4

**Ingredients:**
2 tbsp olive oil
2 tbsp butter, softened
1 lemon, zested and juiced
4 garlic cloves, minced
Salt and black pepper to taste
1 (3 lbs.) whole chicken

**Instructions:**
1. Insert the dripping pan onto the bottom of the air fryer and preheat the device at Roast mode at 400 F for 2 to 3 minutes.
2. In a small bowl, mix the olive oil, butter, lemon zest, lemon juice, garlic, salt, and black pepper. Pat the chicken dry with paper towels and rub the seasoning mix all around and inside the cavity of the chicken. Use cooking twines to tie and secure the wings, legs, and any loose ends into the body of the chicken.
3. Run the rotisserie spit through one open end of the chicken through to the other end and lock the forks with their screws.
4. Lift the chicken, lock the spit onto the lever in the oven and close the lid.
5. Set the timer to 50 minutes and press Start. Cook until the chicken is golden brown all around and the meat tender almost falling off the bone.
6. When done cooking, open the oven and use the rotisserie lift to remove the chicken off the lever.
7. Unscrew, pull out the spit, and allow the chicken sit for 3 to 5 minutes before slicing and serving.

**Nutrition Facts Per Serving**
Calories 296, Total Fat 16.81g, Total Carbs 2.89g, Fiber 0.3g, Protein 32.39g, Sugar 0.91g, Sodium 165mg

# Peri Peri Roasted Chicken

Prep Time: 10 minutes; Cook time: 55 minutes; Serves: 4

## Ingredients:
½ cup olive oil
1/3 cup BBQ sauce
3 tbsp Worcestershire sauce
2 tbsp freshly minced garlic
1 tbsp onion powder
½ lemon, juiced
3 tbsp hot sauce
1 tsp yellow mustard
Salt and black pepper to taste
1 (3 lbs.) whole chicken

## Instructions:
1. Insert the dripping pan onto the bottom of the air fryer and preheat the device at Roast mode at 400 F for 2 to 3 minutes.
2. In a small bowl, mix all the ingredients up to the chicken. Pat the chicken dry with paper towels and with gloves on your hands, rub the marinade all around and inside the cavity of the chicken. Use cooking twines to tie and secure the wings, legs, and any loose ends into the body of the chicken.
3. Run the rotisserie spit through one open end of the chicken through to the other end and lock the forks with their screws.
4. Lift the chicken, lock the spit onto the lever in the oven and close the lid.
5. Set the timer to 50 minutes and press Start. Cook until the chicken is golden brown all around and the meat tender almost falling off the bone.
6. When done cooking, open the oven and use the rotisserie lift to remove the chicken off the lever.
7. Unscrew, pull out the spit, and allow the chicken sit for 3 to 5 minutes before slicing and serving.

## Nutrition Facts Per Serving
Calories 452, Total Fat 31.41g, Total Carbs 9.15g, Fiber 1.2g, Protein 33.15g, Sugar 3.55g, Sodium 506mg

# Chapter 8 Vegetables

## Black Beans Stuffed Zucchini Boats

Prep Time: 10 minutes; Cook time: 12 minutes; Serves: 4

### Ingredients:

2 medium zucchinis

½ tbsp olive oil

1 small yellow onion, chopped

1 small red bell pepper, deseeded and chopped

3 garlic cloves, minced

1 (15 oz) can black beans, drained and rinsed

1 tbsp tamarind sauce

1 tsp onion powder

1 tbsp tomato paste

1 tbsp hot sauce

Salt and cayenne pepper to taste

4 tbsp almond milk

½ tsp smoked paprika

½ tsp cumin powder

1 tbsp rice vinegar

1 tsp brown sugar

1 tbsp chopped fresh parsley

1 cup crumbled vegan cheese

### Instructions:

1. Cut the zucchinis lengthwise in halves, use a teaspoon to scoop out some of the inner pulp of the zucchinis to form boats, and chop the flesh. Brush the zucchinis with some olive oil and set aside.

2. Heat the remaining olive oil in a medium skillet and sauté the onion and bell pepper until softened, 3 minutes. Mix in the garlic and cook until fragrant, 30 seconds.

3. Stir in the reserved zucchini pulp, black beans, tamarind sauce, onion powder, tomato paste, hot sauce, salt, cayenne pepper, almond milk, paprika, cumin powder, vinegar, and brown sugar. Cover and simmer the sauce for 5 minutes or until sauce thickens. Turn the heat off.

4. Insert the dripping pan onto the bottom of the air fryer and preheat at Broil mode at 400 F for 2 to 3 minutes.

5. Place the zucchini boats on the cooking tray, spoon the sauce filling into the boats, top with the parsley, vegan cheese, and slide the tray onto the middle rack of the oven. Close the oven.

6. Set the timer for 2 to 3 minutes, and press Start. Cook until the cheese melts and light golden brown.

7. Remove the food when ready and serve warm.

### Nutritional Facts Per Serving

Calories 200, Total Fat 12.9g, Total Carbs 11.82g, Fiber 3.1g, Protein 11.03g, Sugar 4.07g, Sodium 255mg

# Crispy Broccoli Tots

Prep Time: 15 minutes; Cook time: 10 minutes; Serves: 4

**Ingredients:**
2 small heads broccoli, cut into small florets and steamed
½ cup almond flour
¼ cup flax seed meal
½ tsp garlic powder
½ tsp salt

**Instructions:**
1. Pour all the ingredients into a food processor and blend until smooth. Pour the mixture into a medium bowl. Using your hands, form 18 to 20 tots from the combination and arrange carefully in the rotisserie basket. Close the basket to seal.
2. Insert the dripping pan onto the bottom of the air fryer and preheat at Air Fryer mode at 400 F for 2 to 3 minutes.
3. Once preheated, attach the rotisserie basket to the lever in the oven and close the door.
4. Set the timer for 10 minutes and press Start. Cook until golden brown and compact.
5. Transfer the broccoli tots to serving bowls when ready and serve warm with ketchup.

**Nutritional Facts Per Serving**
Calories 112, Total Fat 2.53g, Total Carbs 14.61g, Fiber 13.6g, Protein 15.97g, Sugar 1.92g, Sodium 456mg

# Easy Grilled Corn on the Cob with Cilantro

Prep Time: 5 minutes; Cook time: 10 minutes; Serves: 4

**Ingredients:**

4 medium corn cobs, husks removed

Vegetable oil for spraying

Salt to taste for topping

1 tsp fresh lemon zest for topping

1 tsp chopped fresh cilantro for topping

**Instructions:**

1. Insert the dripping pan at the bottom of the air fryer and preheat the oven at Air Fry mode at 400 F for 2 to 3 minutes.
2. Lay the corn cobs in the cooking tray, spray with some olive oil on all sides and season with some salt. Slide the tray onto the middle rack of the oven and close the oven.
3. Set the timer for 10 minutes and press Start. Cook until the timer reads to the end while turning the corn every 2 minutes.
4. Once cooked, transfer to a plate and top with the lemon zest and cilantro.
5. Serve immediately.

**Nutritional Facts Per Serving**

Calories 192, Total Fat 4.74g, Total Carbs 38.96g, Fiber 4.6g, Protein 5.43g, Sugar 0.13g, Sodium 9mg

# Sweet Grilled Green Beans

Prep Time: 10 minutes; Cook time: 8 minutes; Serves: 4

**Ingredients:**
1 lb. green beans
1 tbsp honey
1 tbsp olive oil

**Instructions:**
1. Insert the dripping pan at the bottom of the air fryer and preheat the oven at Air Fry mode at 400 F for 2 to 3 minutes.
2. In a medium bowl, mix the green beans, honey, and olive oil. Pour the green beans into the rotisserie basket and close to seal. Attach the rotisserie basket to the lever in the oven and close the door.
3. Set the timer for 8 minutes and press Start. Cook until golden brown and tender.
4. When ready, transfer the green beans to serving bowls and serve immediately.

**Nutritional Facts Per Serving**
Calories 81, Total Fat 3.26g, Total Carbs 12.23g, Fiber 3.1g, Protein 2.09g, Sugar 8,01g, Sodium 7mg

# Buffalo Cauliflower

Prep Time: 10 minutes; Cook time: 10 minutes; Serves: 4

## Ingredients:

1 medium head cauliflower, chopped into 1 ½ -inch florets
3 tbsp hot sauce
3 tbsp nutritional yeast
1 ½ tsp honey
2 tsp canola oil
¼ tsp salt
1 tbsp cornstarch

## Instructions:

1. Insert the dripping pan at the bottom of the air fryer and preheat the oven at Air Fry mode at 400 F for 2 to 3 minutes.
2. Add all the ingredients to a medium bowl and mix well until the cauliflower looks well coated in the seasoning. Transfer the cauliflower to the rotisserie basket and close the lid to seal.
3. Attach the rotisserie basket to the lever in the oven and close the door. Set the timer for 10 minutes and press Start. Cook until golden brown and tender.
4. When ready, transfer the cauliflower to serving bowls and serve immediately.

## Nutritional Facts Per Serving

Calories 101, Total Fat 2.58g, Total Carbs 10.97g, Fiber 2.5g, Protein 4.72g, Sugar 4.91g, Sodium 661mg

# Honey Roasted Brussels Sprouts

Prep Time: 10 minutes + 2 hours marinating; Cook time: 30 minutes; Serves: 4

**Ingredients:**

1 ½ lbs. Brussels sprouts, halved

1 tbsp honey

5 tbsp olive oil

Salt and black pepper to taste

**Instructions:**

1. Insert the dripping pan at the bottom of the air fryer and preheat the oven at Roast mode at 400 F for 2 to 3 minutes.
2. Add all the ingredients to a medium bowl and mix well until the vegetables seem well coated with the seasoning. Transfer to the rotisserie basket and close the lid to seal.
3. Attach the rotisserie basket to the lever in the oven and close the door. Set the timer for 10 minutes, and press Start. Cook until golden brown and tender.
4. When ready, transfer the Brussels sprouts to serving bowls and serve immediately.

**Nutritional Facts Per Serving**

Calories 243, Total Fat 14.41g, Total Carbs 20.61g, Fiber 6.6g, Protein 5.99g, Sugar 8.63g, Sodium 44mg

# Roasted Garden Veggies

Prep Time: 10 minutes; Cook time: 12 minutes; Serves: 4

## Ingredients:

12 oz cherry tomatoes

8 oz baby bella mushrooms, cleaned and ends trimmed

12 oz baby potatoes, scrubbed and halved (optional)

2 medium zucchinis, cut into 1-inch half moons

12 large garlic cloves, peeled

Olive oil for drizzling

½ tbsp dried oregano

1 tsp dried thyme

Salt and black pepper to taste

¼ cup grated Pecorino Romano cheese for garnishing

¼ tsp red chili flakes for topping

## Instructions:

1. Insert the dripping pan at the bottom of the air fryer and preheat the oven at Roast mode at 400 F for 2 to 3 minutes.
2. In a large bowl, mix ingredients up to the cheese and spread the mixture in a 9-inch baking dish.
3. Slide the cooking tray upside down onto the middle rack of the oven, place the dish on top and close the oven.
4. Set the timer for 10 or 12 minutes, and press Start. Cook until the vegetables are tender.
5. Transfer the veggies to a serving platter when ready, garnish with the cheese, red chili flakes, and serve warm.

## Nutrition Facts Per Serving

Calories 333, Total Fat 2.67g, Total Carbs 76.43g, Fiber 10.7g, Protein 10.81g, Sugar 13.5g, Sodium 10mg

# Summer Balsamic Roasted Vegetables

Prep Time: 10 minutes; Cook time: 10 minutes; Serves: 4

## Ingredients:
2 medium zucchinis, cut into 1-inch pieces
1 small red onion, peeled and cut into wedges
1 red bell pepper, deseeded and cut into 1-inch chunks
1 yellow squash, cut into 1-inch pieces
2 tbsp olive oil
1 tsp dried basil
1 tbsp balsamic vinegar
Salt and black pepper to taste
¼ cup chopped fresh parsley

## Instructions:
1. Insert the dripping pan at the bottom of the air fryer and preheat the oven at Roast mode at 400 F for 2 to 3 minutes.
2. In a large bowl, add all the ingredients and spread the mixture in a 9-inch baking dish.
3. Slide the cooking tray upside down onto the middle rack of the oven, place the dish on top and close the oven.
4. Set the timer for 10 minutes, and press Start. Cook until the vegetables are tender.
5. Transfer the veggies to a serving platter when ready and serve warm.

## Nutritional Facts Per Serving
Calories 82, Total Fat 6.9g, Total Carbs 4.87g, Fiber 0.9g, Protein 0.95g, Sugar 2.55g, Sodium 6mg

# Maple Cinnamon Roasted Squash

Prep Time: 10 minutes; Cook time: 10 minutes; Serves: 4

## Ingredients:

3 lbs. butternut squash, peeled and cut into 2-inch cubes
2 tbsp olive oil
2 tbsp maple syrup
½ tsp cinnamon powder
½ tsp salt
2 pinches cayenne pepper

## Instructions:

1. Insert the dripping pan at the bottom of the air fryer and preheat the oven at Roast mode at 400 F for 2 to 3 minutes.
2. Add all the ingredients to a medium bowl and mix well until the squash pieces seem well coated with the seasoning. Transfer to the rotisserie basket and close the lid to seal.
3. Attach the rotisserie basket to the lever in the oven and close the door. Set the timer for 10 minutes, and press Start. Cook until golden brown and tender.
4. When ready, transfer the squash to serving bowls and serve immediately.

## Nutritional Facts Per Serving

Calories 198, Total Fat 7.18g, Total Carbs 35.99g, Fiber 5.4g, Protein 2.79g, Sugar 0.06g, Sodium 10mg

# Simple Air Fried Okra

Prep Time: 10 minutes; Cook time: 10 minutes; Serves: 4

**Ingredients:**
½ lb. okra, ends trimmed and pods sliced
Salt and black pepper to taste
1 tsp olive oil

**Instructions:**
1. Insert the dripping pan at the bottom of the air fryer and preheat the oven at Air Fryer mode at 400 F for 2 to 3 minutes.
2. Add all the ingredients to a medium bowl and mix well. Transfer the okras to the rotisserie basket and close the lid to seal.
3. Attach the rotisserie basket to the lever in the oven and close the door. Set the timer for 10 minutes, and press Start. Cook until golden brown and tender.
4. When ready, transfer the okras to serving bowls and serve immediately.

**Nutritional Facts Per Serving**
Calories 33, Total Fat 1.26g, Total Carbs 5.29g, Fiber 2g, Protein 1.32g, Sugar 1.41g, Sodium 5mg

# Chapter 9 Desserts

## Orange Chocolate Brownies

Prep Time: 10 minutes; Cook time: 40 minutes; Serves: 4

**Ingredients:**
1 cup butter, melted
1 ½ cup dark chocolate, roughly chopped and melted
1 orange, zested
2 ¼ cup granulated sugar
4 large eggs
2/3 cup all-purpose flour
¼ cup cocoa powder
½ cup orange flavored dark chocolate, chopped

**Instructions:**
1. Preheat the oven at Bake mode at 360 F for 2 to 3 minutes, line a 9-inch square cake pan with parchment paper and set aside.
2. In a medium bowl, mix the butter, dark chocolate, and orange zest until smooth. You can do this on a stovetop.
3. In another bowl, using an electric mixer, whisk the sugar and eggs until smooth and fluffy. Gradually, mix in the chocolate mixture until well combined. Sift the flour and cocoa powder into the batter, blend well, and then fold in the orange-flavored chocolate. Pour the mixture into the cake pan.
4. Slide the cooking tray upside down onto the middle rack, set the cake pan on top, and close the oven.
5. Set the timer for 35 to 40 minutes, and press Start. Cook until the cake sets.
6. Remove the cake pan, allow the cake to completely cool in the pan and then, cut into squares.
7. Enjoy afterward.

**Nutritional Facts Per Serving**
Calories 635, Total Fat 55.52g, Total Carbs 25.58g, Fiber 1.8g, Protein 9.76g, Sugar 6.85g, Sodium 81mg

# Tahini Pretzel Cookies

Prep Time: 15 minutes + 45 minutes refrigeration; Cook time: 30 minutes; Serves: 4

## Ingredients:

¼ cup tahini

1 ½ cup unsalted butter

1 ½ cup white chocolate

2 cups all-purpose flour

1 tsp baking soda

2 tbsp toasted sesame seeds + more for garnishing

¼ tsp cinnamon powder

1 cup light brown sugar

½ cup granulated sugar

2 large eggs

2 tsp vanilla extract

½ cup pretzels, broken into small shards

## Instructions:

1. Preheat the air fryer oven at Bake mode at 360 F, line 2 to 3 8-inch cookie sheets with parchment paper, and set aside.
2. Add the tahini and butter to a medium pot, and melt over medium heat with frequent stirring until well combined. Turn the heat off, add the white chocolate (leaving a quarter cup for later use) and mix until the chocolate melts.
3. In a medium bowl, mix the flour, baking soda, sesame seeds, and cinnamon powder. Set aside.
4. In another bowl, combine the brown and granulated sugars, and whisk in the tahini mix. Add the eggs, vanilla, and beat further until the mixture is pale and starts to thicken. Gradually, fold in the dry ingredients until well combined. Pour in the remaining white chocolate, pretzels, and fold in well. Cover the bowl with plastic wrap and refrigerate for 30 to 45 minutes or until firm like ice cream texture.
5. Remove the bowl from the fridge and using an ice cream scoop, fetch pounds of the mixture onto the cookie sheets with 1-inch intervals. Sprinkle some sesame seeds on top.
6. Slide the cooking tray upside down onto the middle rack of the oven, sit one cookie sheet on top and close the lid.
7. Set the timer for 10 minutes and bake until the cookies' edges are brown but the centers still soft.
8. Remove the cookie sheet and place it with another in the oven. Bake in the same manner until all the cookies look thoroughly baked.
9. Transfer the cookies to a wire rack to cool completely and enjoy afterward.

## Nutritional Facts Per Serving

Calories 1179, Total Fat 79.96g, Total Carbs 95.64g, Fiber 4.1g, Protein 19.98g, Sugar 38.26g, Sodium 533mg

# Chocolate Fudge Cake

Prep Time: 10 minutes; Cook time: 20 minutes; Serves: 4

## Ingredients:

1 cup self-raising flour
¼ cup cocoa powder
1 tsp baking powder
1/3 cup brown sugar
1/3 cup softened butter
3 large eggs
1 tsp vanilla extract
4 tbsp dark chocolate, melted

## Instructions:

1. Preheat the oven at Bake mode at 350 F and line 2 8-inch round baking pans with parchment paper. Set aside.
2. Add all the ingredients to a food processor and blend until smooth. Divide and level the mixture between the two cake pans while leaving room on top for rising.
3. Slide the cooking tray onto the middle rack of the oven, place one pan on top and close the oven.
4. Set the timer for 20 minutes and press Start. Cook until the timer reads to the end or until the cake is spongy.
5. Once ready, change the cake pans and bake the other one.
6. Transfer the cakes onto a rack to cool, dress with your preferred frosting if using, slice, and enjoy the cake.

## Nutritional Facts Per Serving

Calories 321, Total Fat 20.35g, Total Carbs 27.25g, Fiber 3g, Protein 9.13g, Sugar 0.69g, Sodium 430mg

# White Chocolate and Peach Cookies

Prep Time: 10 minutes; Cook time: 20 minutes; Serves: 2

## Ingredients:

1/3 cup butter, room temperature

¼ cup brown sugar

½ cup golden caster sugar

1 tsp vanilla extract

1 egg

1 tbsp whole milk

2 cups self-rising flour

1/3 cup white chocolate, roughly chopped

½ cup dried peaches, cut into small pieces

## Instructions:

1. Preheat the oven at Bake mode at 350 F and line two 8-inch cookie sheets with parchment paper. Set aside.
2. In a medium bowl, using an electric mixer, beat the butter and sugars until light and creamy. Crack in the egg, add the milk, vanilla, and beat until smooth. While still whisking, gradually add the flour until well combined and then fold in the white chocolate and peaches.
3. Roll out 1-tbsp balls out of the mixture, sit the balls on the cookie sheet, and use a fork to flatten them slightly.
4. Fix the cooking tray upside down on the middle rack of the oven, place a cookie sheet on top and close the oven.
5. Set the timer for 10 minutes and press Start.
6. Once the timer reads to the end, remove the cookie sheet and bake the other set in the same manner.
7. Transfer the cookies to a wire rack to cool and enjoy after.

## Nutritional Facts Per Serving

Calories 382, Total Fat 16.92g, Total Carbs 48.52g, Fiber 2g, Protein 7.91g, Sugar 2g, Sodium 764mg

# Pear and Salted Caramel Blondies

Prep Time: 10 minutes; Cook time: 33 minutes; Serves: 4

## Ingredients:

½ cup butter

4 tbsp salted caramel + extra for topping

1 cup demerara sugar

2 eggs, beaten

½ cup white chocolate, cut into chunks

2 small pears, peeled, cored and cut into chunks

1 cup self-rising flour

## Instructions:

1. Preheat the oven at Bake mode at 350 F for 2 to 3 minutes and line an 8-inch square cake pan with parchment paper. Set aside.
2. Melt the butter in a medium pot over low heat and mix in the caramel and sugar until melted and golden brown. Turn the heat off and allow cooling to warm, then whisk in the eggs, white chocolate, and pears until well combined.
3. Pour the flour into a medium bowl and mix in the pear mixture until well incorporated. Pour the batter into the cake pan and level the top.
4. Fix the cooking tray upside down on the middle rack of the oven, place the cake pan on top and close the oven.
5. Set the timer for 30 minutes and press Start. Cook until set and golden brown.
6. Remove from the oven, allow cooling, slice, and enjoy.

## Nutritional Facts Per Serving

Calories 513, Total Fat 35.01g, Total Carbs 30.58g, Fiber 3g, Protein 18.9g, Sugar 4.84g, Sodium 548mg

# Assorted Jam Tarts

Prep Time: 10 minutes; Cook time: 15 minutes; Serves: 4

**Ingredients:**
3 cups all-purpose flour
1 ½ cups butter, softened
½ cup golden caster sugar
2 egg yolks
1 orange, zested
Assorted jam for filling

**Instructions:**
1. In a medium bowl, whisk the flour and butter until breadcrumb-like mixture forms. Beat the in the eggs, caster sugar, and orange zest until smooth dough forms. Wrap the dough in plastic wrap and refrigerate for 20 minutes.
2. After 20 minutes, remove and unwrap the dough and using a full-round cookie cutter, stamp out pastry rounds. Fit these round dough pieces into 2 x 12-hole tart tins.
3. Preheat the air fryer at Bake mode at 350 F for 2 to 3 minutes.
4. Working in batches, arrange as many tart tins as possible on the cooking tray, slice the tray onto the middle rack of the oven, and close.
5. Set the timer to 15 minutes and press Start.
6. Remove the tart tins after, empty the tart onto the wire rack to cool and then, fill with the different jam types.
7. Serve afterward.

**Nutritional Facts Per Serving**
Calories 976, Total Fat 71.77g, Total Carbs 71.76g, Fiber 2.5g, Protein 12.8g, Sugar 0.4g, Sodium 38mg

# Salted Honey Brownies

Prep Time: 12 minutes; Cook time: 20 minutes; Serves: 4

## Ingredients:

**For the crust:**
1 ½ cups digestive biscuits, crushed
2 tbsp milk powder
2 tbsp honey
One large pinch salt flakes
2 tbsp butter, melted
2 tbsp heavy cream

**For the filling:**
¼ cup butter
½ cup chopped dark chocolate
2 eggs
½ cup golden caster sugar
¼ cup plain flour
½ tsp baking powder
2 tbsp cocoa powder
2 tbsp honey
Salt flakes to taste

## Instructions:

1. Preheat the oven at Bake mode at 350 F for 2 to 3 minutes and line an 8-inch square cake pan with parchment paper. Set aside.
2. In a medium bowl, mix the digestive biscuits, milk powder, honey, salt flakes, butter, and heavy cream until well combined and holds. Spoon and press the mixture to fit into the bottom of the cake pan.
3. In a medium, safe microwave bowl, add the butter, chocolate, and melt in the microwave until melted. Remove from the microwave, allow slight cooling to warm and one after another, whisk in the eggs, caster sugar, flour, baking powder, cocoa powder, honey, and salt flakes. Pour the mixture onto the crust and level the top.
4. Fix the cooking tray upside down on the middle rack of the oven, place the cake pan on top and close the oven.
5. Set the timer for 20 minutes and press Start. Cook until set and golden brown.
6. Remove from the oven, allow cooling, slice into squares and, enjoy.

## Nutritional Facts Per Serving

Calories 365, Total Fat 24.73g, Total Carbs 32.45g, Fiber 1.8g, Protein 7.31g, Sugar 18.49g, Sodium 171mg

# Almond Butter and Jam Scones

Prep Time: 10 minutes; Cook time: 20 minutes; Serves: 4

## Ingredients:

3 tbsp smooth almond butter
1 cup whole milk
2 2/3 cup self-rising flour + extra for dusting
2/3 cup cold butter, chopped
½ tsp salt
2 tbsp golden caster sugar
1 cup roasted almonds, finely chopped
Seedless berry jam for serving
Clotted cream for serving
Smooth almond butter for serving

## Instructions:

1. Preheat the oven at Bake mode at 350 F for 2 to 3 minutes and line an 8-inch cookie sheet with parchment paper. Set aside.
2. In a medium pot, add the almond butter and milk. Whisk over medium heat until melted and well combined. Turn the heat off and allow cooling to warm - Reserve 2 tablespoons for glazing.
3. In a large mixing bowl, using your hands, mix the flour and butter until breadcrumb-like texture forms. Whisk in the salt, sugar, almonds, and then quickly mix in the milk mixture onto smooth dough forms.
4. Lightly dust a flat surface with some flour, empty the dough on top and knead a few times to get rid of big cracks. Pat the dough into 3cm thickness, dust a 6 cm round cutter with some flour and, cut out rounds of the dough. Set the dough on the cookie sheet with 1-inch intervals and brush the top with the reserved milk mixture.
5. Slide the cookie tray onto the middle rack of the oven, sit the cookie sheet on top, and close the oven.
6. Set the timer for 20 minutes and press Start. Cook until set and golden brown.
7. Remove from the oven, allow cooling, and cut the scones in halves.
8. Spread the jam on top, add the clotted cream, and some almond butter. Serve immediately.

## Nutritional Facts Per Serving

Calories 728, Total Fat 41.06g, Total Carbs 77.02g, Fiber 3.6g, Protein 14.11g, Sugar 12.71g, Sodium 1043mg

# Sticky Maple Cakes

Prep Time: 10 minutes; Cook time: 20 minutes; Serves: 4

**Ingredients:**
1 ½ cups salted butter, very soft
2/3 cup light brown sugar
1 ½ cups maple syrup
2 eggs, beaten
2 cups self-rising flour
1 tbsp freshly squeezed lemon juice
1 tsp ginger powder

**Instructions:**
1. Preheat the oven at Bake mode at 350 F for 2 to 3 minutes and line an 8-holed cupcake tin with parchment paper. Set aside.
2. In a medium bowl, one after the other, as they combine, whisk all the ingredients until smooth. Divide the batter between the cupcake tins while leaving some room on top for rising.
3. Slide the cookie tray upside down onto the middle rack of the oven, sit the cupcake tin on top and close the oven.
4. Set the timer for 20 minutes and press Start. Cook until golden, risen, and springy.
5. Remove from the oven, transfer the cupcakes to a wire rack to cool and serve.

**Nutritional Facts Per Serving**
Calories 864, Total Fat 71.76g, Total Carbs 46.95g, Fiber 1.7g, Protein 9.69g, Sugar 0.37g, Sodium 786mg

# Salted Caramel Shortbread

Prep Time: 10 minutes; Cook time: 20 minutes; Serves: 4

**Ingredients:**
**For the shortbread:**
2 cups butter
1 ½ cups golden caster sugar
¼ cup caramel
3 cups self-rising flour
1 cup rice flour
1 cup chopped dark chocolate
Salt flakes for garnishing

**Instructions:**
1. Preheat the oven at Bake mode at 350 F for 2 to 3 minutes and line an 8-inch cookie sheet with parchment paper. Set aside.
2. In a food processor, beat the butter and caster sugar until light and creamy. Mix and add the remaining ingredients one after another as they combine evenly until smooth dough forms.
3. Lightly dust a flat surface with some flour and knead out the dough and sprinkle with the salt flakes. Fold in half and spread the mixture onto the cookie sheet. Cover with plastic wrap and chill for 30 minutes.
4. After, slide the cooking tray onto the middle rack of the oven, transfer the cookie sheet onto the cooking tray (without the plastic wrap) and close the oven.
5. Set the timer for 20 minutes and press Start. Cook until golden brown.
6. Remove from the oven, allow cooling, cut the shortbread into rectangular pieces, and enjoy.

**Nutritional Facts Per Serving**
Calories 1229, Total Fat 93.83g, Total Carbs 101.36g, Fiber 3.5g, Protein 14.15g, Sugar 0.35g, Sodium 1137mg

# Chapter 10 Snacks

## Mixed Veggie Chips

Prep Time: 20 minutes; Cook time: 9 minutes; Serves: 4

**Ingredients:**
1 zucchini
1 sweet potato peeled
1/2 tsp pepper
1 red beet, peeled
1 large carrot
1 tsp salt
1 tsp Italian seasoning
A pinch cumin powder

**Instructions:**
1. Preheat the air fryer in Dehydrate mode at 110 F for 2 to 3 minutes.
2. Meanwhile, use a mandolin slicer to thinly slice all the vegetables and transfer to a medium bowl. Season with salt, Italian seasoning, and cumin powder.
3. In batches, arrange some of the vegetables in a single layer on the cooking tray.
4. When the device is ready, slide the cooking tray onto the top rack of the oven and close the oven
5. Set the timer to 7 or 9 minutes and press Start. Cook until the vegetables are crispy.
6. Transfer the vegetables to serving bowls when ready and make the remaining in the same manner. Enjoy.

**Nutrition Facts Per Serving**
Calories 84, Total Fat 0.15g, Total Carbs 18.88g, Fiber 2.7g, Protein 2.25g, Sugar 1.94g, Sodium 652mg

# Sweet Apple and Pear Chips

Prep Time: 15 minutes; Cook time: 7 minutes; Serves: 4

**Ingredients:**

6 Honeycrisp apples

6 pears, peeled

**Instructions:**

1. Preheat the air fryer in Dehydrate mode at 110 F for 2 to 3 minutes.
2. Meanwhile, use a mandolin slicer to thinly slice the apples and pears.
3. In batches, arrange some of the fruit slices in a single layer on the cooking tray.
4. When the device is ready, slide the cooking tray onto the top rack of the oven and close the oven
5. Set the timer to 7 minutes and press Start. Cook until the fruits are crispy.
6. Transfer the fruit chips to serving bowls when ready and make the remaining in the same manner. Enjoy.

**Nutrition Facts Per Serving**

Calories 142, Total Fat 0.46g, Total Carbs 37.7g, Fiber 6.6g, Protein 0.71g, Sugar 28.36g, Sodium 3mg

# Cocoa Banana Chips

Prep Time: 5 minutes; Cook time: 7 minutes; Serves: 4

**Ingredients:**

5 large firm banana, peeled

¼ tsp cocoa powder

A pinch of cinnamon powder

**Instructions:**

1. Preheat the air fryer in Dehydrate mode at 110 F for 2 to 3 minutes.
2. Meanwhile, use a mandolin slicer to thinly slice the bananas, and coat well with the cocoa powder and the cinnamon powder.
3. In batches, arrange as many banana slices as possible in a single layer on the cooking tray.
4. When the device is ready, slide the cooking tray onto the top rack of the oven and close the oven
5. Set the timer to 7 minutes and press Start. Cook until the banana pieces are crispy.
6. Transfer the chips to serving bowls when ready and make the remaining in the same manner. Enjoy.

**Nutrition Facts Per Serving**

Calories 152, Total Fat 0.57g, Total Carbs 38.89g, Fiber 4.4g, Protein 1.87g, Sugar 20.79g, Sodium 2mg

# Coriander Roasted Chickpeas

Prep Time: 10 minutes; Cook time: 45 minutes; Serves: 2

**Ingredients:**

1 (15 oz) can chickpeas, drained
1/4 tsp ground coriander
1/4 tsp curry powder
1/4 tsp garlic powder
1/4 tsp ground cumin
1/4 tsp paprika
1/8 tsp salt
1/4 tsp chili pepper powder
Olive oil for spraying

**Instructions:**

1. Preheat the oven in Air Fryer mode at 375 F for 2 to 3 minutes.
2. In a medium bowl, mix the chickpeas with all the spices until well combined and pour into the rotisserie basket. Grease lightly with olive oil, shake the basket, and close the seal.
3. Fix the basket onto the lever in the oven and close the oven.
4. Set the timer to 35 or 45 minutes, press Start and cook until the chickpeas are golden brown.
5. After, open the oven, take out the basket using the rotisserie lift and transfer the snack into serving bowls.
6. Allow cooling and enjoy.

**Nutrition Facts Per Serving**

Calories 91, Total Fat 1.82g, Total Carbs 14.87g, Fiber 4.2g, Protein 4.61g, Sugar 2.71g, Sodium 234mg

# Parmesan Zucchini Chips

Prep Time: 15 minutes; Cook time: 7 minutes; Serves: 4

**Ingredients:**
3 medium zucchinis
Salt to taste
1 cup grated Parmesan cheese

**Instructions:**
1. Preheat the oven in Air Fryer mode at 110 F for 2 to 3 minutes.
2. Meanwhile, use a mandolin slicer to thinly slice the zucchinis, season with salt, and coat well with the Parmesan cheese.
3. In batches, arrange as many zucchini pieces as possible in a single layer on the cooking tray.
4. When the device is ready, slide the cooking tray onto the top rack of the oven and close the oven.
5. Set the timer to 7 minutes and press Start. Cook until the cheese melts while turning the halfway.
6. Transfer the chips to serving bowls to cool and make the remaining.
7. Serve warm.

**Nutrition Facts Per Serving**
Calories 107, Total Fat 6.99g, Total Carbs 3.73g, Fiber 0.1g, Protein 7.33g, Sugar 0.02g, Sodium 451mg

# Ranch Garlic Pretzels

Prep Time: 10 minutes; Cook time: 15 minutes; Serves: 4

**Ingredients:**

2 cups pretzles
½ tsp garlic powder
1 ½ tsp ranch dressing mix
1 tbsp melted butter

**Instructions:**

1. Preheat the oven in Air Fryer mode at 270 F for 2 to 3 minutes.
2. In a medium bowl, mix all the ingredients until well combined, pour into the rotisserie basket and close to seal.
3. Fix the basket onto the lever in the oven and close the oven.
4. Set the timer to 15 minutes, press Start and cook until the pretzels are lightly browner.
5. After, open the oven, take out the basket using the rotisserie lift and transfer the snack into serving bowls.
6. Allow cooling and enjoy.

**Nutrition Facts Per Serving**

Calories 35, Total Fat 3.72g, Total Carbs 0.4g, Fiber 0g, Protein 0.12g, Sugar 0.1g, Sodium 40mg

# Herby Sweet Potato Chips

Prep Time: 12 minutes; Cook time: 7 minutes; Serves: 4

## Ingredients:
2 medium sweet potatoes, peeled
1 tsp dried mixed herbs
1 tbsp olive oil

## Instructions:
1. Preheat the oven in Air Fry mode at 375 F for 2 to 3 minutes.
2. Meanwhile, use a mandolin slicer to thinly slice the sweet potatoes, transfer to a medium bowl and mix well with the herbs and olive oil until well coated.
3. In batches, arrange as many sweet potato slices as possible in a single layer on the cooking tray.
4. When the device is ready, slide the cooking tray onto the top rack of the oven and close the oven.
5. Set the timer to 7 minutes and press Start. Cook until the sweet potatoes are crispy while turning halfway.
6. Transfer the chips to serving bowls when ready and make the remaining in the same manner. Enjoy.

## Nutrition Facts Per Serving
Calories 87, Total Fat 3.48g, Total Carbs 13.38g, Fiber 1.9g, Protein 1.03g, Sugar 4.33g, Sodium 20mg

# Cumin Tortilla Chips with Guacamole

Prep Time: 5 minutes; Cook time: 15 minutes; Serves: 4

## Ingredients:
For the tortilla chips:
12 corn tortillas
2 tbsp olive oil
1 tbsp cumin powder
1 tbsp paprika powder
Salt and black pepper to taste

## For the guacamole:
1 large avocado, pitted and peeled
1 small firm tomato, chopped
A pinch dried parsley

## Instructions:
1. Preheat the oven in Air Fry mode at 375 F for 2 to 3 minutes.
2. In a medium bowl, mix all the ingredients for the tortilla chips well and pour the mixture into the rotisserie basket. Close to seal.
3. Fix the basket onto the lever in the oven and close the oven.
4. Set the timer to 15 minutes, press Start and cook until the tortillas are golden brown.
5. After, open the oven, take out the basket using the rotisserie lift and transfer the chips to serving bowls.
6. Meanwhile, as the chips cooked, in a small bowl, mash the avocados and mix with the tomato and parsley until well combined.
7. Serve the tortilla chips with the guacamole.

## Nutrition Facts Per Serving
Calories 159, Total Fat 14.74g, Total Carbs 7.82g, Fiber 4.6g, Protein 1.94g, Sugar 1.71g, Sodium 9mg

# Oven-Dried Strawberries

Prep Time: 10 minutes; Cook time: 7 minutes; Serves: 4

**Ingredients:**

1 lb. large strawberries

**Instructions:**

1. Preheat the air fryer in Dehydrate mode at 110 F for 2 to 3 minutes.
2. Meanwhile, use a mandolin slicer to thinly slice the strawberries.
3. In batches, arrange some of the strawberry slices in a single layer on the cooking tray.
4. When the device is ready, slide the cooking tray onto the top rack of the oven and close the oven
5. Set the timer to 7 minutes and press Start. Cook until the fruits are crispy.
6. Transfer the fruit chips to serving bowls when ready and make the remaining in the same manner. Enjoy.

**Nutrition Facts Per Serving**

Calories 36, Total Fat 0.34g, Total Carbs 8.71g, Fiber 2.3g, Protein 0.76g, Sugar 5.55g, Sodium 1mg

# Chili Cheese Toasts

Prep Time: 5 minutes; Cook time: 8 minutes; Serves: 4

**Ingredients:**

6 slices sandwich bread
4 tbsp butter
1 cup grated cheddar cheese
2 small fresh red chili, deseeded and minced
½ tsp salt
1 tsp garlic powder
1 tsp red chili flakes
1 tbsp chopped fresh parsley

**Instructions:**

1. Preheat the oven in Broil mode at 375 F for 2 to 3 minutes.
2. Spread the butter on one side of each bread slices and lay on a clean, flat surface.
3. Divide the cheddar cheese on top and followed with the remaining ingredients.
4. Lay 3 pieces of the bread on the cooking tray, slide the tray onto the middle rack of the oven, and close the oven.
5. Set the timer for 3 to 4 minutes and press Start. Cook until the cheese melts and is golden brown on top.
6. Remove the first batch when ready and prepare the other three bread pieces.
7. Slice the into triangle halves and serve immediately.

**Nutrition Facts Per Serving**

Calories 105, Total Fat 11.53g, Total Carbs 0.68g, Fiber 0.1g, Protein 0.29g, Sugar 0.04g, Sodium 388mg